EMBER

943

making her some
nd thonged with
ttern, of course.

the A.T.S. . . . but
ave-times, made by
braid.

of the ordinary—my
and surprise them—
dance in.

bswool soles—they're
got an up-and-down-
you see.

ssy things—so I'm seeing
ever, slip-into bedroom
d from wool left-overs.

S, BUT WE CAN STILL TURN OUT
MENT YOU'LL FIND DIRECTIONS
HOWN HERE.

COLD MEAT
And How To
DISGUISE IT

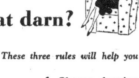

COLD MEAT
And How To
DISGUISE IT

A History of Advice on How to Survive Hard Times:
A Hundred Years of Belt Tightening

HUNTER DAVIES

F

FRANCES LINCOLN LIMITED

PUBLISHERS

Frances Lincoln Ltd
4 Torriano Mews
Torriano Avenue,
London NW5 2RZ
www.franceslincoln.com

A catalogue record for this book is
available from the British Library

ISBN 978-0-7112-3051-4

Printed in Slovenia

9 8 7 6 5 4 3 2 1

No Hoarding: A Fair Share for Everybody

The Government is endeavouring to
see that every person has a fair share of
food and it is therefore of the greatest
importance that every member of the
public should assist in maintaining a
fair distribution of supplies. They
should do this by refraining from buying
more than their usual quantities of foodstuffs.

Retailers should co-operate in secur-
ing a fair distribution of their stocks.

Bakers generally are holding satisfactory stocks of flour and coal.

The Executive Committee, appointed
by the London Division Exchange,
unanimously agreed that all market
prices established on Friday last for all
kinds of butter, cheese, bacon, ham, and
lard shall remain the maximum prices
until further notice.

In some parts of the provinces there
seems to be an inclination to put up
prices, partly caused by a certain amount
of panic buying, which, however, is
being checked by the traders and Co-
operative Societies themselves.

Some fish has been sent to London
from Lowestoft by sea.

Milk services are being well maintained.

National Food Journal, 13 March 1918

INDEX

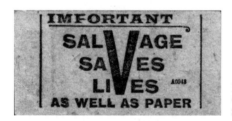

East Kent Road Car
Company ticket,
Second World War

ACKNOWLEDGMENTS

All the illustrations used in this book are taken from my own
collections of books, newspapers, magazines, leaflets, posters,
postcards and other assorted original treasures of the period.
Where possible, exact dates and sources are given. I'd like to
thank and apologise to all those artists, authors, copywriters,
designers – many of them long gone, unnamed and unknown –
whose excellent work I have used. Also a thank you to
Michael Brunström for knocking it all into shape – HD

INTRODUCTION

The gastro pub round the corner from me, the Bull and Last, is advertising 'sprats burgers'. Not tried them yet, and probably never will, for in my mind sprats are about the lowest form of fishy life, only used by end-of-the-pier fishermen as bait when they can afford nothing else.

Waitrose, which is supposedly the most expensive, upmarket supermarket, patronised by people who don't look at prices, has introduced pigs' trotters and bath chaps to its shelves. Traditionally, they were considered the poorest, cheapest part of the pig, bought by poor persons oop north or in the more deprived parts of London's east end. Bath chaps, by the way, come from the pig's cheek as opposed to trotters, which are the feet, complete with toenails if you're not careful.

Food prices rocketed in 2008, up 40 per cent in some cases, so we were all conscious of trying to keep our bills down, by eating cheaper stuff we might not have contemplated before, cooking cheaper meals, going to cheaper places, avoiding too much waste or just eating less.

Petrol prices, they zoomed up as well, so we were being encouraged to drive less or, more economically, get on our bikes or, best of all, start walking again.

We're currently in hard economic times, as bad as the 1930s, so the experts tell us; awful crashes and crunches have happened on a global scale to banks, mortgages, investment, credit, oh everything financial really, hence all classes are being urged to make economies.

The Queen has been facing a cash crisis over the rising costs of her staff and palaces, and wants more help. A man has had his £11 million mansion in Holland Park repossessed because he couldn't pay his mortgage. Lots of reasons why, of course, none of which makes one's heart bleed, but it shows it can now happen to anyone, up or down the financial scale.

It therefore behoves us to tighten the old belt, be careful with our money and resources, make do and mend, spin things out, count the pennies, do as much as we can to save, save, save.

In this particular period in our glorious history, we are at the same time being exhorted to save the planet – reduce our carbon footprints, conserve fuels and energies, go green, live a sustainable life. So walking to save money on fuel and transport will not just help our pockets, but the planet. And also, of course, our bellies.

Despite the fact that so many more families are becoming hard up, and economic and social poverty increasing, there's also the irony that obesity is now a national concern. Seems strange that if times are hard we should be getting fatter – unlike in the war when we all got thin – but apparently it's partly to do with the poor and deprived spending what little money they have on cheap, junk, easy, convenient, fattening food, instead of the healthy stuff like fruit and veg, and of course not taking enough exercise.

So from all sides, for lots of different reasons, from

governments to agony aunts, we are being cajoled and bombarded – to eat sensibly, live economically, save money, save energy, waste not want not.

'Twas ever thus, of course. We've been here before. Lots of times. If not always brought about by the same reasons and causes, concerns or conditions as we are facing today.

Looking back over the last hundred years or so, we can see much the same sorts of advice and warnings, guidance and suggestions being given out – not just by governments of the time but household manuals, domestic goddesses and clever manufacturers, all of them supposedly concerned about our welfare, encouraging us to save.

During two world wars, of course, it was imperative that we made the most of what little we had, living on rations, doing clever things with parsnips, reusing and reheating, disguising leftovers. Fortunately, today, as I speak, we are not at war, circumstances are different, but in some ways there is a similar need and desire to save and conserve what we have. A lot of those old tips, hints and exhortations seem funny and amusing today. In some cases they are now totally irrelevant and mystifying as life has moved on. All of them, however, are informative, giving us an insight into past social conditions and economic situations.

There are also quite a few which are in fact quite useful today. You never know, you might find it very helpful to know how to knit old bits of string in order to make a dishcloth, or turn leftover cold scraps into a succulent new dish.

London, 2009

MEAL TIME NOVELTIES
FOR BUSY HOUSEWIVES
by Marjorie Gully

New ways of serving the same old dishes

MONEY SAVING
TIME SAVING
HEALTH SAVING
NOURISHING PLEASING
THE NECESSARY
VITAMIN "B"

Will please the whole family!

1 FOOD

Saving on food and using up scraps have always been among the most obvious ways to economise – and literally tighten one's belt. It doesn't take a war or economic crisis to make most sensible people aware that they shouldn't be chucking away perfectly good food just because too much was made, people have had enough or it's gone all horrible, greasy, yucky, nasty and cold.

In the past, that didn't happen all that much, as even in well-off families there was a long tradition of children being forced to eat up. They had to chew every piece of grizzle, swallow it if necessary, finish off all their tripe and tapioca, no use saying you don't like it, think of all the starving hordes in Africa. Every plate had to be left clean, otherwise that was it, straight to bed. Oh, that was the way to bring up children. No mess, no messing around.

The lack of a fridge or freezer was another reason for trying to avoid having leftover food. Houses did have cold stores, ingenious larders which kept stuff reasonably fresh and useable, but not for very long in hot weather. There was a continual fear and dread of being lumbered with a great pile of

Meal Time Novelties for Busy Housewives, 1920s

KITCHEN MAXIMS
'Save all pieces of fat to melt down for frying or pastry.'
'Put spare crusts in the oven to grate for breadcrumbs.'
'Pare potatoes thinly.'
'One egg well beaten is worth two not beaten.'
Mrs Beeton's All About Cookery, 1920s

leftovers, when so much time and money and resources had been spent buying or preparing it, so cooks and housewives were always on the look out for good ideas.

In the earliest editions of Mrs Beeton's cookery books – which first appeared in 1861 and continued to come out long after she had died in 1865, aged only twenty-eight – there were always sections on 'The Art of Using-Up'. She also offered labour-saving advice, tips on how to make renovations, plus information on legal and health matters where they concerned the home.

One of her hints, which appeared in other books of the time, was how to cook with a hay box. You could actually buy these special hay boxes and follow Mrs Beeton's directions for 'Hay-Box or Fuelless Cookery'. It wasn't quite fuelless, despite the title, as you had to semi-cook the stew, or whatever, before putting it in the hay box where it continued to simmer for several hours.

There was also a vogue, around the end of the nineteenth century, for 'paper bag cookery'. I feel that could catch on today, as it sounds ecologically sound, with no carbon footprints or fossil fuel waste, and presumably dead cheap. I've read the instructions for doing this, but still haven't quite got the hang

Cold Meat and How to Disguise It, 1904

of it. It appears you had to grease the paper bag first, inside and out, then make it watertight, which sounds a bit of faff. Best not to try it at home.

There were also complete books devoted to leftovers. My favourite is *Cold Meat and How to Disguise It,* and not just because of its excellent title and attractive cover. It was published in 1904 by Arthur Pearson and written by M.E. Rattray. No clue to his or her sex but according to the title page he/she had a First Class Diploma from the National Training School of Cookery in London, and was also the author of *Sweetmeat Making at Home.*

She, for we might as well presume she was a she, offers no-nonsense hints in a very school-mistressly manner. 'A person of average intelligence can easily learn how to make a great variety of dishes from the remains of cooked joints, providing she understands the arts of broiling, frying and making simple savoury sauces and, above all, is careful never to allow previously cooked meat to reach the heat of boiling water (212°F), for

BREAD SOUP

Fry two onions in a saucepan with a little lard, add a pint of water and three slices of bread cut rather thick. Season with pepper and salt, and boil for ten minutes.

The Best Way Book, 1914

Dainty Dishes for Slender Incomes, 1895

this will immediately render it hard, unpalatable and indigestible.' Still sound advice today.

She takes us through the different ways to use up cold beef, chicken, veal and pork, making use of every scrap, turning them into tasty rissoles, croquets and scallops. By scallops she didn't mean scallops as we know them today. The word referred to the dish, shaped like a scallop shell, in which you cooked and served the disguised leftovers. Perhaps a quick or hungry eater did imagine he was having real scallops and not just some chopped up old pork covered with one of her twenty-five

---

R 1.—(January).

MINISTRY OF FOOD.

PURCHASER'S SHOPPING CARD.

This Card is valid only with the Retailer who issued it and whose name appears below. If you change your Retailer, the latter must issue a new card, and you must return this card to the Food Office.

A. RETAILER'S NAME AND ADDRESS.

The Retailer must stamp his name and address below before issue, otherwise the card will not be valid.

```
MAYPOLE DAIRY Co LTD
77 HIGH ROAD,
BALHAM, S.W
```

B. PURCHASER'S NAME AND ADDRESS.

Mrs Chas Crons

103 Entisham Rd

Balham S.W.

THIS CARD IS VALID ONLY WITH THE RETAILER WITH WHOM THE HOLDER IS REGISTERED.

(29049) W:. /2819 18,500,000 11-19 W B & L

First World War ration card

recipes for savoury sauces. They in fact were her main secret for disguising.

Once the First World War started, and rationing came in, using up leftovers became a full-time occupation for everyone. I hadn't realised just how serious it all was until I came across a Ministry of Food journal issued in March 1918 and discovered that an actual law had been passed which made it illegal to waste food. The head of the house could be sent to prison if he allowed foodstuffs to be wasted in his household. Later in the same journal, there is a list of people who had been prosecuted under the Waste of Foodstuffs Order.

I also hadn't been aware of a fearsome sounding committee called the National Salvage Board, which was encouraging all organisations, such as the army, to recover fat from all possible sources in their kitchens and canteens. Fat had to be collected from the sides of soliders' plates, after they'd finished, and washing up water had to be skimmed to catch any floating fat. Then it was all reused. Ugh. At least our present government hasn't gone that far, though I suppose it could happen, once the City of London totally collapses, all banks close, five million unemployed, and no one can afford to drive a car or buy any food. Then we'll all have to live on leftovers.

During that war, most newspapers and magazines had recipes for economical meals. Then after the war, there were special features aimed at 'War Brides', helping them to cope in the kitchen. In 1919, a magazine called *Good Luck* ran a series called 'War Bride's Cookery Book' which was to help young

BRIDES!

You cannot afford to miss this splendid weekly feature.

Remember—

A good breakfast means a good day's work.

A bright fire in winter, and a cool, shady room in summer, with a neatly-laid table.

See tea is freshly made ; butter and marmalade in clean dishes ; and have one tempting, fizzlingly-hot dish. Don't forget a pot of ferns or a few flowers.

Be punctual.

But be merciful, if anyone is late down. Do your best to keep things hot ; don't **nag** and tell " him " it's his own fault it's all cold.

Get ready overnight all you can possible.

MENU.

Tea.	Brown bread-and-butter.
Baked eggs with ham.	Watercress.

The above would make a delicious and sustaining breakfast.

'War Brides' Cookery Book', *Good Luck*, 24 May 1919

women who had spent the last four years in factories making munitions, but had now suddenly got married to their boyfriend back from the front, if they were lucky, without having had any experience of cooking. 'No wonder you find preparation of the daily meals a big trial, you poor little war brides. You have not had the chance of picking up housekeeping in the usual way, but read these articles, written specially for you, and you will find your difficulties vanishing like smoke.'

The first recipe was for tea. You know, making a cup of tea. Hard to believe in 1919 there were women to whom this was a mystery, but that was apparently the case. The second recipe was for eggs with ham. 'This Series will make your homes hospitable and your husbands happy!'

In the Second World War, rationing was more intense, better organised, started earlier and lasted longer. The government had had a fright back in 1917 when at one point it was realised the country was only six weeks from total starvation. This time contingency plans were being made from the mid-1930s onwards, in case anything awful happened, in order to make sure the whole population would be fed as equally and nutritionally as possible.

Food rationing was introduced in 1940, followed by clothes rationing, and rationing in some form went on until the mid-1950s. Bread, fish, offal and vegetables were not on 'coupons', as rations were called, and were usually available, in season, but almost every other item of food, such as sugar, tea, butter, margarine, cheese, jam and sweets, were all strictly limited to around 1–8 ounces per week per person.

Substitutes appeared, such as dried eggs, and the Ministry of Food encouraged people to experiment with food they had never tried before, such as nettles, dock leaves, whale meat, or using parts of the animals which had formerly been ignored, such as

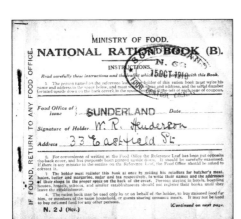

First World War
ration book

By order of the Ministry of Food only one main dish and one subsidiary dish or two subsidiary dishes may be served at any single meal. Subsidiary dishes are starred and main dishes printed in Red

Dejeuner au Choix

*Hors d'Œuvre Riche

ou

Consommé Double Brésilien   Crème Bagration

*Spaghetti au Goût du Chef

ou

Moules Poulette   Salade de Crabe

LES PLATS DU JOUR :

La Truite Saumonée Froide Moscovite

Le Darne de Cabillaud à la Russe

Le Suprême de Barbue Marguery

Le Sauté de Veau Provençale
Stewed Veal with Mushrooms, Tomatoes and Olives

Le Steak and Vegetable Pie
Steak Pie with Paysanne of New Vegetables

La Cervelle en Fritôt Orly
Fried Calf's Brains, Tomato Sauce

Salade de Saison

Petits Pois	Haricots Verts Frais	Epinards à la Crème
Carottes Vichy	Chouxfleur	Choux de Bruxelles
Pommes Persillées	Nature	Purée

Entremets Parisien

Owing to the prohibition of Cream by the Ministry of Food, a substitute
(Vita-Cream) will be served if desired

Second World
War menu,
Mayfair Hotel,
London,
2 April 1942

'Dried Eggs', War Cookery Leaflet 11, Ministry of Food, c.1940

sheep heads or brains. The government gave out recipes and Lord Woolton, who became Minister of Food in 1940, introduced us to imaginative dishes including roast turkey, without actually using any turkey, cakes without sugar, tea without any tea leaves. His best-known recipe, which in fact had been created by the Savoy Hotel's chef, but became known as Woolton Pie, consisted mainly of carrots.

Woolton Pie was mocked, featured in radio comedians' jokes and sketches, but in a way Woolton Pie was treated affectionately by the long-suffering public. They quite liked Lord Woolton and acknowledged he was doing a good job in bad times.

The Illustrated London News, 16 February 1946

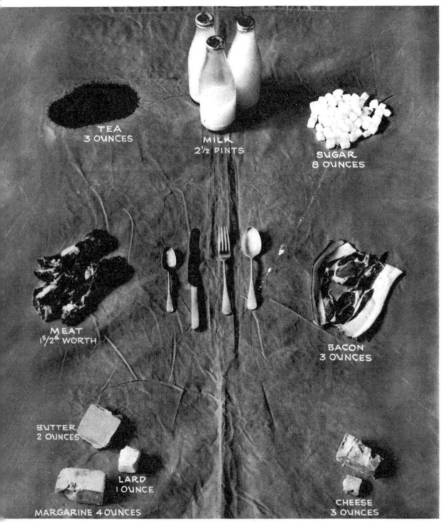

TEA
3 OUNCES

MILK
2½ PINTS

SUGAR
8 OUNCES

MEAT
1 5/2ᵈ WORTH

BACON
3 OUNCES

BUTTER
2 OUNCES

LARD
1 OUNCE

MARGARINE 4 OUNCES

CHEESE
3 OUNCES

OUR illustration above shows the items of rationed food available to one British civilian for one week, and it provides striking evidence of the austerity being suffered by the people of Britain to-day. Bread and vegetables remain unrationed, as also does fish. Other items of food, mostly canned, are obtainable by the points rationing system; i.e., 24 points per person for a four-week period. Four additional points will be available on March 3 next. The Minister of Food, Sir Ben Smith, announced in the House of Commons last week a reduction in the fats ration by 1 oz. from March 3; a return to the darker wartime loaf; less feeding-stuffs for animals, and therefore shorter supplies of bacon, poultry and eggs; and a restriction on the serving of bread in restaurants. Sir Ben Smith explained that the shortage of cereals, mainly wheat and rice, had been largely brought about by droughts in Australia, the Argentine, North Africa and South Africa. Failure of the rains, and other disasters in India, make it clear that India will be faced with the prospect of famine. Thus, all importing countries [Continued on right.

COMMODITY	JUNE 1942	FEBRUARY 1946	COMMODITY	POINTS VALUE JUNE 1942	POINTS VALUE FEBRUARY 1946
Bacon	4 ozs.	3 ozs.	AMERICAN MEATS	24-32	UNOBTAINABLE
Sugar	8 ozs.	8 ozs.	SALMON	32	32
			SARDINES	24 per lb	10 per lb
Tea	2 ozs.	3 ozs.	PILCHARDS	12 per lb	4 per lb
			HERRINGS	6 per lb	2 per lb
Meat	1/2 ᵈ	1/2 ᵈ	SULTANAS	12 per lb	8 per lb
Cheese	4 ozs.	3 ozs.	TINNED MILK	4-8	4-8
			RICE	4	UNOBTAINABLE
			BAKED BEANS	4	4
Preserves	1 lb.	1 lb.	BISCUITS	UNRATIONED	2-4 per lb
			SUET	UNRATIONED	†
Fats	8 ozs.	7 ozs. ★			

★ From 3ʳᵈ March 1946
† On Points 3ʳᵈ March 1946

[Continued.]
will have to make heavy sacrifices. The British Government has taken the lead in accepting a reduction of nearly 250,000 tons in the United Kingdom wheat imports for the first half of 1946. This reduction will have to be met by making greater use for direct human consumption of our wheat supplies, necessitating an early increase in the flour extraction rate to 85 per cent., although this, in itself, may not be the last step we shall have to take. The change will mean a return to the darker wartime loaf, but there will be no deterioration in the nutritive value of our bread, although it will materially reduce the volume of animal feeding-stuffs, and, in consequence, will result in a diminution of livestock production in this country. This will mean less bacon, poultry and eggs. The tabulation (left) shows how quantities of the principal rationed and points foods have changed to-day compared with June 1942. With regard to the item "Preserves," it should be stated that 1 lb. (jam, marmalade, or sugar in lieu if desired) has to last four weeks, whereas the other items are weekly rations.

RICH FARE BLESSED
BY LORD WOOLTON

Lord Woolton's Department suggests: – 'Mock turkey, made from 2½–3 lbs of stewing steak, cut into slices, and held on either side by piles of stuffing, to make the 'body' of the 'turkey', served with a few grilled sausages in place of the legs. The pudding, cooked the same day, to be minus eggs, although egg substitute can be used. Apples, carrots and potatoes to be included, to add to the dried fruits, and lemon flavouring, instead of lemon or orange peel. Coffee or cocoa can be used to flavour of colour. Instead of Christmas fruits, prunes, stewed for 24 hours, stoned and chopped fine.'

Lilliput, January 1943

It was interesting to see a feature in the *Independent* in September 2008, at the beginning of the present-day credit crunch, which gave readers recipes for some old wartime dishes. The writer of the article, Clare Rudebeck, had come across a scrapbook of recipes kept by her granny during the 1940s. They included Giblet Pie and Corned Beef Balls, both of which she tried out. She failed at first to find any chicken giblets. Her local butcher explained that today all his chickens came ready cleaned, all their innards, such as liver, stomach, liver, long since removed. She managed to get some at a farmers' market. Corned beef was easier to find, and she got a tin from her local supermarket. The only problem was opening it. A tin of corned beef (which

POTATOES

THERE is no vegetable more useful than the homely potato It is a valuable yet cheap source of energy, and one of the foods that help to protect us from ill-health. It contains vitamin C as do oranges and 1-lb. of potatoes daily will give half the amount of this vitamin needed to prevent against fatigue and help fight infection.

So don't think of potatoes merely as something to serve with the meat. They can be much more than that. A stuffed baked potato can be a course in itself. Potatoes can be used, too, in soups, salads, pastry, savoury supper dishes and even biscuits, as the following recipes show.

'Potaotes', Ministry of Food Leaflet 27, 1946

In 1943, according to the Ministry of Information, the country was now eating 27 per cent less fresh meat than before the war, 56 per cent fewer shell eggs, 36 per cent less butter but 54 per cent more potatoes. There were no bananas and no white bread in Britain.

doesn't actually contain corn but is the less desirable parts of a cow, ground up very small) was always hard to open. The key was usually attached, and had to be turned the right way in the right place, and got easily broken or lost. But

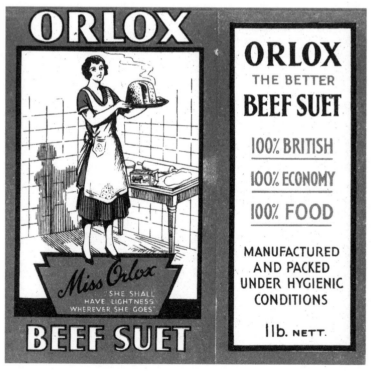

Orlox Beef Suet packaging, early 1920s

..Shoot straight, Lady

You've got a fighting job on hand, too. These are significant days and anyone — man, woman, or child — who is less than fighting fit is a pull back on the total war effort.

FOOD is your munition of war. The Government sees that you get the right stuff and it's vital that you should know how to use it to full advantage . . .

There's cheese : it makes muscle and bone.
There are potatoes : they give energy and warmth.
Carrots, that give vitality and help you to see in the dark.
Green vegetables, with their valuable salts and vitamins, which are so important for clear complexions and sound teeth.

Did you know that 5 quarts of summer milk — milk at its richest and when it is most plentiful — go to the making of 1 lb. cheese ?
Or that swedes, the juice of which you used to give to babies because of its valuable Vitamin C, are now to be had at most greengrocers cheap enough and in big enough quantities for you to serve as a second or third vegetable to the entire family.

All good live stuff. And you need them all : *every day.* Serve everything appetisingly as you so well can do. Then you can be proud of your vital, active part in the drive to Victory.

CHEESE SOUP

Ingredients . 1½ oz. margarine, 2 tablespoonfuls flour, 2 tablespoonfuls chopped onion or leek if possible, 2 cups water, 2 cups household milk, 1 cup grated cheese, 2 tablespoonfuls chopped parsley, salt and pepper. *Method :* Add onion and margarine to milk and water, bring to the boil, cook for 15 minutes, *stirring all the time.* (Remember household milk catches more easily than ordinary milk, so stirring is important.) Blend flour with a little milk, stir in and cook for a few minutes to thicken. Add cheese and seasoning. Stir until the cheese is melted but do not boil again. Add parsley and serve very hot.

LOBSCOUSE

A quickly-made dish, very popular with sailors. You'll like it, too ! Melt a nut of margarine in a small saucepan, then add 3 oz. grated cheese and about 2 tablespoonfuls milk. Stir over a low heat until the cheese is melting, then add two or three tinned or bottled tomatoes, cut in pieces, and continue to cook gently until all ingredients are blended.

Season with pepper and salt. Serve on a bed of piping hot mashed potato.

POTATO FINGERS

Mix 1 oz. flour with ½ lb. mashed potato, with salt and pepper. Bind, if necessary, with a little milk, or reconstituted dried egg. Shape into fingers, glaze with egg or milk, bake in a hot oven for about 10 minutes until brown and crisp.

A CHRISTMAS GIFT

Everyone, grown-up or child, who has to take packed lunches, craves for a good *hot* lunch now and then, and therefore would welcome the gift of a portable hay-box. Soup, stew, sausage and mash, shepherd's pie, or any other favourite dish keeps *really* hot in this box, for several hours. You can make the portable hay-box from a spare gas-mask carrier. It's very simple. Full directions will be sent if you write to the Ministry of Food, Room 629K, London, W.1.

ISSUED BY THE **MF** MINISTRY OF FOOD
(S52)

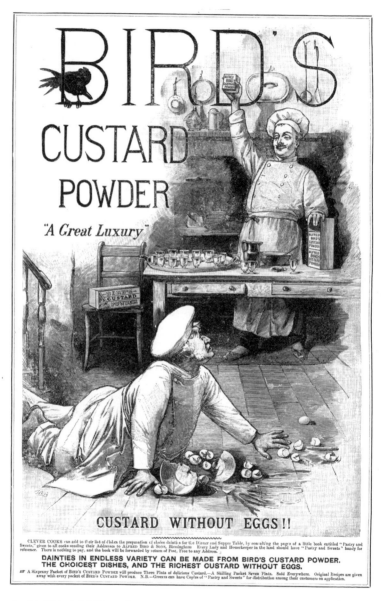

Lady's Pictorial, 7 December 1889

LARK PIE

Take the bones out of the birds. Line a pie-dish with a nice light crust, put in some farce, then the birds, and more farce on top to fill up the dish; close the pie, leaving a hole at the top. Bake to a light brown colour; then remove the crust, pour in a little chicken broth, season highly, and serve.

Recipes for the Million, 1891

she made both dishes and appeared to enjoy them.

The packet of giblets cost her 50p while the tin of corned beef was only £1.16. Excellent. That's what I like to hear. Bring back all the old wartime recipes, I say, and you'll save a fortune.

Sheep's Head Broth

1 sheep's head	1 turnip
3 qts. cold water	1 onion, if possible
2 tablespoonfuls pearl barley	2 sticks celery
2 carrots	pepper and salt
1 tablespoonful chopped parsley	

Ask your butcher to dress and clean the head for you and be sure that he sends you the brains and the tongue.

Take out the brains and save for sauce or a separate savoury. Wash the head and tongue thoroughly and let them soak in cold water with a handful of salt in it, for an hour or more. Then put the head and tongue in a large saucepan with cold water to cover them and a little salt, bring to the boil, pour this water away and rinse the head and the saucepan with clean water. Put the head back into the saucepan with the barley, a little salt and three-quarts of cold water. Bring to the boil and skim well. Add the turnip, carrot, onion and celery cut into neat pieces. Simmer slowly for 3½ hours. Add the parsley at the last, with pepper and more salt, if necessary. (Enough for 5 or 6).

The head may be lifted out and served as a separate dish with parsley or brain sauce poured over it. Or, as much as seems desirable of the meat may be cut in small pieces and served in the soup. The tongue should always be skinned before being used.

Ministry of Food War Cookery leaflet 2, *c*.1940

WHAT YOU SHOULD KNOW ABOUT ELECTRIC COOKING

NO WASTE OF FOOD OR FUEL
MORE NOURISHING MEALS
KEEPS DOWN EXPENSE – WAR OR PEACE
CONSTANTLY CLEAN
EASIER, "CONTROLLED" COOKING

There's no waste—either of food or fuel. Electric cooking preserves the nourishment and flavour of food. There's no wasteful "guesswork" cooking. Everything is controlled. You switch on and leave the meal to the electric cooker. You switch off before the dish is finished — controlled heat finishes it off.

Electric cooking is extraordinarily clean — and cheap. It costs only about 1 unit per person per day. Go to your Electricity *Show*rooms for free and friendly information and for help in your wartime kitchen and cooking problems — there is no obligation.

ELECTRIC COOKING
Wages War on Waste!

BRITISH ELECTRICAL DEVELOPMENT ASSOCIATION, 2, SAVOY HILL, LONDON, W.C.2

2 DOMESTIC

It has to be said, though not by me, as I do nothing in our house, that there can be a definite satisfaction in domestic labour. I once had a fireside chat with my dear wife, over the cocoa, in which we wondered what we'd do if we both fell on hard times and no one would employ us. I said I'd have a market stall, or a car boot table, and try to sell some of my treasures, a bit of this, a bit of that. She said she'd go out cleaning. She wouldn't find it demeaning or embarrassing, in fact she would quite enjoy it. Funny woman.

'Lily-white and clean, oh!' sang Beatrix Potter's Mrs Tiggy-Winkle, happily extolling the virtues of washing, drying and ironing. There's no doubt there is pride to be had in making a good job of keeping one's house, mud hut or cave gleaming and sparkling. And of course watching someone else doing the domestic chores can be even more satisfying – and possibly exciting. 'Dashing away with the smoothing iron, she stole my heart away.'

But over the centuries, any woman with any sense – and it's always been women's lot, not the other lot's lot – has yearned to have easier, quicker, different, cheaper ways of doing their domestic chores.

From 'Simple Vegetable Cooking', Royal Horticultural Society, 1940

From 'Simple Vegetable Cooking', Royal Horticultural Society, 1940

To answer their cries for help, and of course make a lot of money, there has always been a stream of new ways, new methods, new technologies, which promise they have cracked it, solved the problem, even when you were not aware there was a problem. Amazing new inventions, from pot hooks to microwave ovens, are usually either bigger or better, cheaper or quicker, and definitely going to provide wonderful savings.

Such changes and developments have come along all the time on the domestic front, not only during periods of temporary belt tightening caused by wars, acts of God or economic disasters, but when times are generally hard, money short, labour limited.

Cooking is the most basic domestic function. It was around long before dusting the pelmets, polishing the windows, arranging the flowers, sorting the recycling bins. You have to eat before you can do anything else. Raw food is fine, very good for you, but it gets a bit boring and limited. Finding some way to heat up the raw stuff, transform it, make it palatable, that's the clever part.

Historically, cooking has emerged in many stages, but the interesting thing about it – in contrast to many other fields of human development – is that the ancient methods never disappeared. New ways came in, as they always do, but in cooking, the old ways have carried on, give or take a few adaptations, ending up sitting side by side with the modern, providing another string to the cook's bow, another part of her portfolio.

The oldest form of cooking was roasting – shoving something over a fire. Next came boiling – shoving food and water in a sort of container and hanging it over a fire to heat up. Then came the first variations and developments on both themes.

Spit roasting, for example. What a brilliant idea that was. Hanging the dead bird or animal on some sort of spit over the fire did away with all that nasty burning, with the stuff inside still raw and the outside charcoal. Once you'd worked out a way of turning and controlling the joint at regular intervals, you

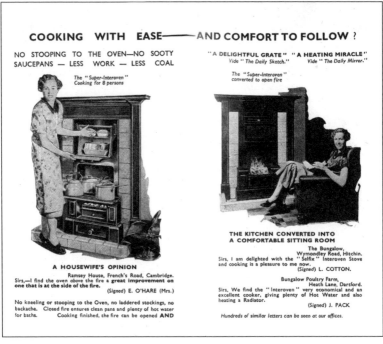

From an advert for 'The Interoven Stove', 1930s.

could also put a pan underneath and capture all that delicious dripping. With boiling, the advances came with improved iron pots and kettles and clever pot hooks to suspend the pots and the required height.

Baking, that probably came in very early as well, once it was discovered that mixing flour and water could be turned into something really quite acceptable by laying it flat on slabs of hot stone. Bannocks, or similar, were born. The next stage was an enclosed area, heated from outside, where the same baking action took place, or ovens as we now call them.

From the eighteenth century, we began to get ranges – specially constructed iron grates, built into the front of the fire, on which cooking utensils could be placed and left to cook. The heat at first was still produced in much the same way as in the past, by either wood or later coal, but the arrival of the range did make cooking a little easier and cleaner to control.

If you look at illustrations of early kitchen ranges, you can see them reflected in modern stoves – with similar sorts of grids, grills and different functions, even though today the designs materials and source of heat are so different. Except for, of course, the aga. That's hardly changed in 200 years.

The coming of gas was a big revolution. The first gas domestic stoves or cookers appeared in general use in the 1880s. Before that, gas had been seen purely as an industrial tool, for factories and street lighting. Gas totally changed cooking. Fuel, in the shape of wood or coal, did not have to be carted into the house and stored. No need to get up early to light the fire, keep it stoked all day, then clean up the mess and dirt every night. You could control gas, unlike wood, decide on the degree of heat, stop and start it when you wanted. Your gas cooker was used only for cooking, nothing else, unlike the old-fashioned kitchen range where the fire was also a source of heat and hot water.

Electric cookers came in a bit later, and were not really in popular use till the 1920s. As with gas, electricity was originally only used industrially, but when gas started to enter the nation's

COMPTON MACKENZIE
cooks for £5 A YEAR

COMPTON MACKENZIE SAYS: "*The Aga which was installed in my house on the island of Barra two years ago has burnt steadily night and day ever since. The economy of it is incredible. The luxury of it is exquisite. My Siamese cats consider the top, covered with a blanket, provides them with the finest lodging outside Siam.*"

Good Housekeeping, April 1938

kitchens, electricity realised it had to follow. The competition between gas and electricity meant that in the 1920s and 1930s there was a constant stream of new models and inventions. The various manufacturers boasted how cheap they were to run, how they boiled water faster and cheaper than anything else on the market.

One Thousand
RISKS A YEAR
• • •

INVEST in an Electrolux refrigerator and your food will be as safe as the Bank of England.

This is an extract from an advertisement of a group of Gas Companies in the Swindon area, and it prompts the thought, in our minds, of the "dividends" that such an investment brings.

The housewife thinks of food in terms of three meals a day. But to appreciate the importance of food and health protection it is wiser to remember that each member of the household having three meals a day consumes over 1,000 meals a year. Three health risks a day and a thousand risks a year—per person. *It needs only one of those risks to actualise* and it may mean serious illness—indeed a fatality, as the newspapers frequently prove.

The housewife should take this wise and sensible viewpoint when thinking of cost. The actual cost of a refrigerator, say an LFG, over a life of ten years, is about 3d. or 4d. a day, including running costs. Surely that is a magnificent investment—a wonderfully cheap insurance premium *for the whole family*. No investment could be wiser; none will pay better dividends.

Electrolux Gas Refrigeration Monthly, October 1936

The main selling points were speed, labour saving, cleanliness and, of course, cost. Modern woman, especially in times of economic depression or war, wanted to save in every way possible, be it pennies or minutes.

It's often imagined that servants were doing much of the

WITH ONLY ONE MAID

Can you give me some advice about the best way for one maid to wait at table? How can one avoid meat getting steadily colder before the vegetables are served? The maid stands by my husband as he carves, and takes all the plates to the guests before serving the vegetables (the guests sit and wait!) This is a problem I cannot solve.

'Be Socially Well-Graced: Lady Troubridge Will Help You With Your Everyday Problems', *My Home*, July 1938

dreary, drudgy domestic work until quite recent times. When growing up in the 1950s, I did sometimes meet people of an ordinary middle class persuasion who quite surprised me when I learned that they had a live-in maid, despite having only a rather modest four-bedroom, detached house in the suburbs. It seemed to them quite normal. Pre-war, of course, such a house would have had several servants, at least that's how it was in Just William's home.

In fact, the heyday of the live-in servant was the Victorian age, and things were never quite the same again after the First World War. During that war, 400,000 women and girls had left domestic service to go into factory work. After the war, many never went back, refused to go back, or were incapable of going back. They didn't know about domestic service, just as they couldn't make a pot of tea, never having been trained to do it. A similar effect was felt after the Second World War.

People's Friend, 9 November 1940

After the war the middle class wealthy preferred to put their money into goods, such as cars or holidays, while at the same time families grew smaller in size, compared with Victorian times.

Servants proved harder to get and to keep, and mistresses began to feel they had a responsibility to make their hours shorter, their labour less arduous and monotonous.

Manufacturers in their early, pre-war advertisements pointed out how their new devices would ease the load on the poor

The Ministry of Information in 1942 reported that only standardised 'utility' furniture was now being made, which had to conform to specific economy measurements and designs, and was available only for urgent needs – such as newlyweds or people bombed out of their own house. Linen sheets were no longer being made, nor were tablecloths.

servants. The Daisy vacuum cleaner was said to be so efficient in removing dirt from your whole house that a housemaid and a boy could do it – thus saving you the need to employ outside help.

In recent decades, we have mostly all got used to non-servant households. Dailies might come in to help women with their busy lives, or au pairs with children, but you rarely hear of anyone employing a cook today. Why would anyone need one, with our wonderful modern cookers which can be remote controlled, or microwaves which can heat food in seconds? Plus all the ready-made meals or pizzas or curries which can be delivered to the door. We've also got instant hot water, dish washing machines, fridges and freezers.

We've now been saved from domestic drudgery, haven't we? Even in hard times, things have been made easier in the kitchen. As long of course as we have the money.

Time is what we all want these days That's what we'd *really* like to save.

From 'Simple Vegetable Cooking', Royal Horticultural Society, 1940

CARRY ON, CASSEROLES!

the clear oven glass

MAKE THE VERY BEST of your war-time rations by cooking and serving them in Phoenix clear glass dishes. The flavour of home-grown fruit and vegetables is improved when cooked "en casserole." All their high nutritive value is retained, and they look much more attractive and appetising. Remember, too, that you can dish up in smart Phoenix dishes, straight from the oven, piping hot, to the table—so Phoenix saves a lot of washing up!

PHOENIX
REGD. TRADE MARK

THE CLEAR GLASS OVENWARE
"For cooking the most economical way"

Free illustrated catalogue:— Dept. V., Phoenix Works, Loxdale Street, Bilston, Staffs

Van Houten's Cocoa

The Nursery.

The Nursery is the training ground of the future generation. Whether the manhood and womanhood of the next decade will be physically and mentally healthy and vigorous depends largely upon the manner in which the children are fed. Mothers should therefore remember that there is no beverage equal to Van Houten's Cocoa for promoting health, strength and good digestion. It is rich in food value, easily digested and most economical in use. Its exquisite natural flavor makes it the favourite beverage for old and young alike.

3 CHILDREN

What to do with children when times are hard, money short, has always been a problem. Sitting them in front of the telly, buying them another computer game, then stuffing their angelic little faces with a Big Mac often proves an excellent solution today, and can be vouched to work by caring parents of all classes. But if you haven't got a telly, because either you can't afford one, they've taken it away or it has not yet been invented, then what do you do?

Children, bless 'em, can amuse themselves for hours with very little more than a saucepan lid and a wooden spoon. We all know that. It worked for my children and I'm sure it will work for yours. The trouble is they don't remain eighteen months old for ever. What happens then? In the past, the moneyed or leisured classes had nurseries and nannies. Off you go, darlings, to the west wing; see you next year. The working classes just opened their front door, straight on to the cobbles, where the young 'uns played till dark, as happy as the day was long.

Gone, all gone, are these rosy solutions. The nanny went when Lehman Brothers collapsed. There are three Polish lodgers in what was once the nursery. As for letting them roam the streets, every reader of the tabloids knows that's inviting trouble.

From *The Illustratred Sporting and Dramatic News*, 12 March 1904

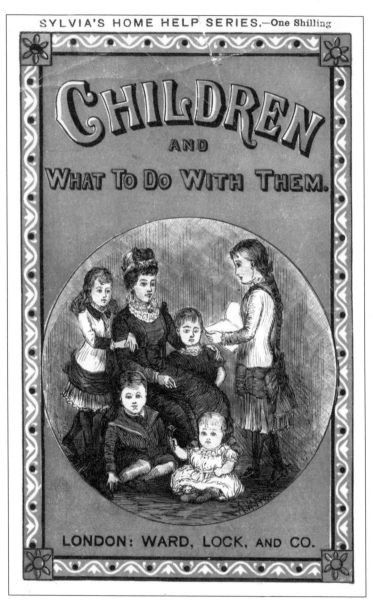

*Children and What To Do With Them, c.*1881

TINKLE TINKLE
**In this game all the players are blindfolded
except one, whom it is their object to catch. The
unblindfolded player must carry a little bell which
tinkles with every movement of the body, thus
revealing his or her whereabouts to the other
players, who are all making frantic efforts to catch
the holder of the bell.**
Indoor Games for Children and Young People, 1912

One of the big problems in the past, for all classes, was being stuck indoors with the children when the weather was foul. The upper classes might have space and staff, but the nannies still had to find ways of amusing the young ones.

A whole industry grew up suggesting ways and means for children to be amused, or to amuse themselves, with the minimum of expenditure. These games and diversions did not require complicated technology. They could be done with, well, nothing much, just a bit of ingenuity and perhaps a piece of string.

During war or hard economic times, books and magazines went to even greater lengths to think up cheap ways to amuse children. Yet while ways to save food and fuel in these tough times have all come back, for some reasons we are not yet being urged to economise on our kids. Try to stop them being obese, yes, we're always being told that – but desist from spending so much money amusing them, that hasn't quite happened yet.

But it will, it will. In preparation, here are some grand ideas from 1912 to amuse the children – without spending a penny.

NURSERY FOOTBALL

Football can be made grandly exciting in the nursery if played in a realistic way, as is possible if you follow these directions. Take an ordinary hen's egg and blow it, by making a small hole at each end and blowing through one hole until all the inside of the egg has been forced into a cup at the opposite end. When this has been done, paint the empty shell as nearly leather-colour as possible with water-colours. When it is dry draw with pen and ink the sections and lacing so as to make it look as much as possible like a real football. Now erect your goal-posts. Four stools will answer the purpose quite well, or even chairs, although the latter are apt to get rather in the way. As in ordinary football the players divide into sides, the object of the game to get as many goals as possible. The ball (or rather egg-shell) is blown across the floor by means of palm-leaf fans. Great care must be taken not to tread upon the ball in the excitement of the game. The score is carefully kept by the umpire, the ball being returned to the centre after each fresh goal.

Indoor Games for Children and Young People, 1912

All 'Nursery Football' needs is a hen's egg. It doesn't say whether the hen should have been free-range, organic, farmers' market, Waitrose or Lidl, class 1, 2 or 3, but don't let that worry you. Any egg will do, but try not to make too much mess. As for blowing the egg, if you find this confusing and you have a granny, ask her nicely and I'm sure she'll show you. That's what grannies used to be for in the good old days – teaching you how to suck eggs.

WINDOW GAMES

If there are two or three of you, the best plan is to divide into sides, Then, if there are two windows, one side can take one window, and one the other. One side must take all the articles passing up the road, and the other everything going in the opposite direction.

If you see:

A man carrying a parcel	you score	5
A man carrying a baby	"	10
A baby in a perambulator	"	8
A sweep	"	10
A white horse	"	20
A woman in an apron	"	30
A butcher's cart	"	6
A piebald horse	"	50
Two children walking hand in hand	"	18
A woman on a bicycle	"	5
A woman on horseback	"	10

If you see:

A woman carrying a parcel	you lose	5
A woman carrying a baby	"	10
A baby walking	"	8
A tinker	"	10
A black horse	"	20
A child with a hoop	"	50
A postman	"	5
A policeman	"	10
A man on a bicycle	"	5
A man on horseback	"	10

No mater which way he may be walking, the side who first sees a soldier wins the game.

Indoor Games for Children and Young People, 1912

Window games can be played with absolutely nothing, not even a piece of string, and will provide endless fun and amusement on a wet day without even the need to go outside. Obviously some of the ways of scoring points will have to be updated, but this can easily be done. 'Someone injecting themselves' can replace, for example, a sweep. Notice what sight means you have won the whole game. Well, it was 1912, a very patriotic period.

Let's not forget that older people might also like to join in a spot of free amusement. *Indoor Games for Children and Young*

People also had a section on how to amuse guests after a dinner party. Instead of passing round nasty drugs, which might well happen today, until they got so frightfully expensive, they suggest two capital diversions: The Lemon Pig and The Inquisitive Banana.

Indoor Games for Children and Young People, 1912

THE LEMON PIG

In order construct this noble creature you must select a lemon with a very decided knob or crease at the norrow end. This forms the head and neck of the pig. Procure two black pins or two grapstones and insert to represent eyes, and with a sharp penknife cut the rind of the fruit to form the mouth and ears. Then take four matches – lucifers are the best, but ordinary wooden ones answer the purpose almost as well – and screw them into the body to form legs, and the animal is complete.

THE INQUISITIVE BANANA

Procure an empty spirit bottle (the ordinary quart size), then take a banana, peel it, and inform the company that you will make the banana go into the bottle of its own accord without breaking either the bottle or the fruit. If the bottle is quite dry you must pour a few drops of spirit into it but as a rule you will find some of the dregs of the spirit still remaining. To these dregs apply a lighted match or taper, and then as soon as the air in the bottle has had time to get hot (a few seconds suffices) place the popint of the banana in the neck of the bottle and steady it until you feel it gradually being sucked in. Then let go and the fruit will enter the bottle, almost imperceiptibly at first, but gradually increasing in momentum until finally, as the air get hotter, it will be drawn right into the bottle with a rush.

Indoor Games for Children and Young People, 1912

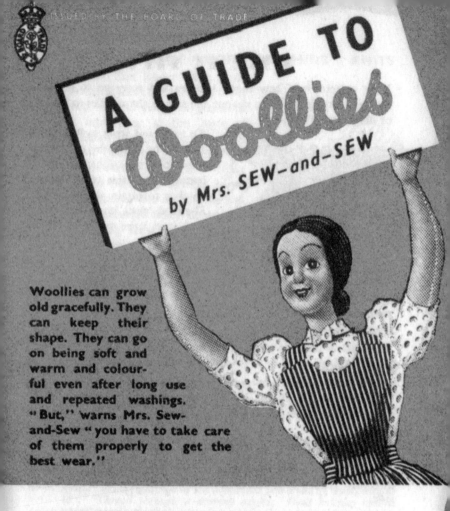

A GUIDE TO Woollies
by Mrs. SEW-and-SEW

Woollies can grow old gracefully. They can keep their shape. They can go on being soft and warm and colourful even after long use and repeated washings. "But," warns Mrs. Sew-and-Sew "you have to take care of them properly to get the best wear."

FIRST STEPS

If wool is not guaranteed pre-shrunk, wash skeins in fairly hot soap suds. Rinse thoroughly. Peg on clothes line away from heat or sun. Shake frequently while drying. Wind into loose balls so as not to strain wool.

TO JOIN WOOL

Join ends in wool by knotting at end of row, by knitting about 2 inches of new piece together with end of last piece or by darning end of last piece about 2 inches into new knitting with darning needle. Avoid knots in the middle of a row.

4 CLOTHING

I can remember clothes rationing during the last war but, as a boy, it didn't really bother me much. I had a pair of very itchy trousers that drove me mad and, looking back, they were probably made of some very cheap utility cloth, possibly old sacking or straw. I also had a suit I hated, a sort of chocolatey brown colour, but the reason I hated it was because it looked like the prison uniform some local Italian prisoners of war wore and at school kids used to shout Eyetie at me.

But of course for women, and especially mothers, clothes rationing was a constant struggle and irritation as they tried to look smart, clean, fresh and also, by some miracle, vaguely fashionable.

During the First World War there was no clothes rationing, but there were shortages and people didn't have much money to spend on new or expensive clothes. In the 2 November 1914 issue of that cosy magazine for women, still going strong today, *People's Friend*, there was a page of patterns for blouses, skirts and sundries addressed to 'Miss Small Purse', which might be thought rather insulting today.

According to an ancient urban myth, hems rise and fall as

'Mrs Sew-and-Sew', Board of Trade leaflet, *c.*1940

the stock markets rise and fall. In the 1930s, hems fell and skirts got longer while in the 1960s they got shorter and shorter. However during the 1940s, when times were bad all round, hemlines were in fact a bit shorter than they had been before the war – that's when you could see hemlines, as so many women were in trousers and dungarees.

Stopping expenditure on fripperies is common in hard times, and in autumn 1930 in the USA, even the Sears catalogue declared that 'thrift is the sprit of the day. Reckless spending is a thing of the past.' However, girls do want to have fun, and feel good, regardless of the current climate. George Orwell summed it up well in 1937: 'The girl who leaves school and gets a dead end job can still look like a fashion plate for a pittance. You may not have a prospect in the world, and only a leaky bedroom to go home to, but in your new clothes, you can stand on the street corner, indulging in a private dream of yourself as Marlene Dietrich.'

People's Friend, 2 November 1914

For Miss ..
Small Purse.

A Tailor-Made Blouse.

THE first of these blouses is one of the new tailor-mades, which will be very fashionable as the season advances. It has a wide armhole, and will look well made up in one of the new woollen materials, the vest and roll collar being of white or a contrasting colour.

Paper Pattern, No. 337, 6½d post free.

We cannot afford to spend too much on clothes this winter for there are many calls on our purses, but here are some designs especially drawn up for the girl whose purse is not too well filled.

A Useful Autumn Skirt.

FOR wear under a sports coat or as a house skirt nothing could be better than this skirt design, as it is simple and neat, and quite the easiest style for dressmaking that could be found. It is all made in one piece, therefore the seam in front is the only one. It ought to be just ankle-length, as obviously it cannot be wide at the hem, and also the style of it is not suited for a long skirt. Serge, tweed, fringe, or heavy cloth are all good materials, and very little is required, but it must be at least 52 inches in width.

2½ yards material, 52 inches wide, at 2s per yard—4s 6d.

Paper Pattern, No. 339, 6½d post free.

In the Second World War, clothes rationing started on 1 June 1941 and lasted until 1949. It came in overnight and people were forced to wear the clothes they already had in their wardrobe and could only buy new ones if they had the right coupons. The choice was limited and material and style very poor. It started at about a hundred coupons per person per year and by 1945 had fallen as low as thirty-six. A woman's coat required fourteen coupons, a frock eleven, pyjamas eight, shoes five, a scarf two, stockings two, so you can see that in any one year it was impossible to buy more than two or three new items.

STOCKINGS

Stockings are an expensive item in a family unless home-made. In every economical house the knitting-basket should be an institution, and all the girls should be taught to knit. Knitted woollen stockings are not only more durable than bought stockings, but they promote the circulation better, and so are a preventive of cold feet and chilblains.

BOOTS AND SHOES

Boots and shoes are a most important consideration in the expenditure of the dress-allowance. There is no economy in buying cheap, inferior, ill-made boots, the health so greatly depends upon the feet being well clad. Many cases of serious illness trace their origin to 'getting the feet wet'. Hand-sewn boots are the best, though the most expensive. Patent leather should be avoided. Good plain leather, calf or kid, is the most durable.

Domestic Economy, 1896

The available stockings were all thick, heavy and made of some sort of cotton rayon and were universally hated. When going out, young women would tan their legs with brown gravy powder and draw a line up the back of their legs with an eyebrow pencil, pretending they were real nylons. Should of course they chance to sweat during some energetic jitterbugging

or while dancing the black and white sergeant, then there was a trickle down their legs and a pool of brown liquid left on the dance floor.

Now and again, ex-army blankets would come into the shops at £1 each and be eagerly snapped up. They would then be

Second World War clothing books

dyed some gay colour and turned into coats and jackets by clever seamstresses. All the women's magazines gave hints and patterns and advice for adding ingenious patches, bits of embroidery, fancy buttons, in order to disguise or transform some worn and boring old article of clothing.

The magazine *Home Notes* for 27 November 1943 devoted a double page spread to a list of suggested Christmas presents, such as new gloves for mother, a shoulder bag for your best girlfriend, a novelty necklace for your sister, lamb's wool sandals for your aunt, bedroom bootees for cousin – and *all* of these items were to be home made. Over the page, it gave exact instructions for making every item. Later on in the same issue there were instructions for adding frills to existing clothes which had become tired looking and making them really new and exciting.

Woman magazine in December 1945 had a notice issued by the Board of Trade which gave useful rules for darning: 'Don't wait for a – darn early and largely.' Knitting of course was a national pastime and

Home Notes,
27 November 1943

Home Notes, 27 November 1943

women seemed to do it almost full time, while talking, eating or listening to the radio.

I was taught to darn and sew on buttons, which I can still do to this day, and also to knit, but I've forgotten how to do that. At primary school, during the war, the whole class would be set the task, both boys and girls, of knitting woollen squares which the teacher would then stitch together to make blankets which were sent to our brave soldiers at the front to keep them warm. I felt sorry for the poor sods who ended up with any blankets I had helped to knit as all my squares were full of holes.

Knitted garments were endlessly recycled – the wool being carefully unpicked, wound into balls then reknitted into a new garment.

The Board of Trade put out a regular series of leaflets giving people advice on darning, sewing, how to repair knickers, make your own slippers, use old parachute nylon, how to smarten up the men in your life, mostly featuring a doll-like cartoon character called Mrs Sew-and-Sew. Quite a good joke name.

> **PUTTING ON FRILLS**
>
> **Your frocks have all got that tired look and you're wondering what you can do for them before 'he' comes home on leave again? Have you thought of frilling? You can either buy it ready-made, it's coupon-free, or else you can make it yourself.**
> *Home Notes*, 27 November, 1943

In 1943 they issued a very useful 34-page booklet called 'Make Do And Mend', which had some excellent suggestions on making clothes last longer, repairing, renovating, washing and ironing. There was a particularly detailed section on caring for corsets and what to do with corset bones when they broke. No, you didn't have to eat them or render them down for fat – they were made of some sort of plastic or metal – but keep them to repair other corsets. It may seem surprising today, when corsets have disappeared and few women under fifty have ever worn them, that with a war on, and so many women in factories dressed in overalls and baggy trousers, so much space was devoted to getting the best out of your corsets.

Advice was also given about what to do about worn underarms – cut out the offending bit and replace it – and also

'Make Do And Mend', 1943

about worn camiknickers and too-tight underwear – all terrific advice for any period.

One of the most ingenious sections was how to turn men's clothing into women's clothing – again this could be very useful in some circles today.

You couldn't get leather-soled shoes and most shoes bought with coupons had wooden soles or what appeared to be cardboard, so they fell to pieces when it rained. Husbands mended shoes with new patches or put on clegs, which were bits of metal to make them last longer. I did at one time wear wooden clogs, which were incredibly hardwearing, but weighed a ton. One advantage of them, to hard-pressed mums, was that they did not require coupons.

In *Woman* magazine for 21 February 1946, a reader writes that she has some very smart black suede court shoes but after two evenings dancing, the toes had been trodden bald. What should she do? She solved the problem by cutting a square of

CORSETS

Now that rubber is so scarce your corset is one of your most precious possessions. Be sure first of all that it fits. In particular, don't wear one too small, as this stretches the rubber and puts too much strain on it. Bones worn in the wrong place – either too high or too low – will break. The greatest enemies of rubber are sunlight and grease. Never let your girdle get really dirty. Wash it frequently, and, if you possibly can, have at least two corsets, and wear them alternately.

MEN'S CLOTHING INTO WOMEN'S

Here are some ways in which a man's unwanted garments can be converted to your own use, if you are quite sure he won't want them again after the war. A pin-striped light suit provides ample material for a tailored frock. Have it made with a yoke and perhaps a front panel, letting the stripes run in different directions. This will look very smart.
A tweed jacket could be cut down to your own measurements and you could then wear it with a flannel skirt and a gay pullover.
Plus-fours will make you an excellent skirt.
'Make Do And Mend', 1943

leather out of an old belt and sticking it on to the toes of her shoes. Bingo. Everyone asked her where she'd got the lovely new shoes from.

There was, of course, a black market, especially for things like nylons. One of the reasons for the great attraction of US soldiers was not just their looks and money, their chewing gum

CUTTING-DOWN
FOR THE CHILDREN

Bathing wraps can be made into children's dressing gowns.
Grey flannel trousers will make children's knickers and skirts.
Plus-fours would make two pairs of shorts for a schoolboy.
Pyjama legs will make children's vests.
An old skirt will make one pair of knickers and a little
play-skirt for a seven-year-old.
Washing-silk dresses make up into gay pyjamas for children.
Woollen stockings with worn feet can have the legs opened
down the back seams and can then be made up into an
infant's jersey. Bind it with ribbon at neck, sleeves and hem.

'Make Do And Mend', 1943

and their nice uniforms (unlike the rough stuff our Tommies had to wear) but their access to nylons. There were girls who would do anything for real nylons – and very often they did.

Brides, of course, had a terrible struggle getting any sort of decent new clothes and new materials, so friends and families rallied round and let the bride-to-be have their coupons. Hair clips were also hard to get, and safety pins had also disappeared from the shops, but almost every household had a sewing machine, or knew someone in the street who was a whiz at running up new garments or altering old ones.

New hats were impossible to find so women resorted to various forms of turbans. This had started in factories, covering their hair while working, then became common in everyday wear. Overalls could be bought without the need for clothing coupons and they became if not popular then commonplace, again an overspill from factory uniforms. Trousers, or slacks, had been worn by some women before the war for smart leisurewear, but became worn by women of all classes during the war. No need for nylons or gravy legs if you wore long trousers.

I hadn't realised till I started collecting wartime documents and leaflets, that there were was such a thing as utility braces. All men, of all classses, wore braces when wearing trousers, especially their best suit – but boys of course didn't. They just had a little elasticated stripey belt, usually with a snake metal buckle, to keep up their short trousers. It would seem that the braces became restricted when war began, and under government rules, the maximum wholesale and retail prices were fixed. Standardised utility braces came in, made of some cheap and nasty material, so fashion-conscious men, as well as fashion-conscious women, did have it hard during the war.

Today, you hardly ever come across homes with sewing machines, or women sitting with darning mushrooms and balls of wool repairing a bundle of holey woollen socks. For forty years, we have got used to socks made of artificial fibres which get thrown away should a hole ever appear. Clothes now get discarded once worn and patches never get applied to elbows any more.

In these harder economic times, clothes making and clothes repairing does not as yet appear to have returned on any great scale – but what has happened is the huge increase in people

sock your slippers!

If you can knit a sock and stitch a sole, these smart and cosy slipper-socks are yours for the making

A pair of strong soles and some knitting wool combine to make these extra-cosy house slippers for winter

Woman, week ending 29 December 1945

wearing second-hand clothes. Women, even in fashionable areas, who for years gave all their often perfectly good clothes to charity shops, have now returned to these shops to pick up bargains to wear themselves. All charity shops selling old clothes have seen an upsurge in sales.

Personally, I have used charity shops for years, for things like jackets, as well as for books and other items, of course, so I am not all pleased by all these posh women cluttering up my local Oxfam and Save the Children, fighting over the goods.

Many of these charity shops can easily turn over £100,000 a year – most of it sheer profit, which upsets rival shops, especially bookshops, who have to buy their stock, pay staff and pay full local council taxes. Charity shops do in fact pay proper commercial rentals, but not council taxes, as they are charities. They rely on volunteer staff, though some of the bigger shops have a paid manager.

I visited a Save the Children shop in Penrith the other day and was allowed into their private upstairs room where donated clothes are cleaned using a steam press and then sorted. I discovered they put a secret code on all clothes so they know how long each garment has been on show. Seventy per cent goes in the first week, and most of the rest in another week. After two weeks, they could reduce the prices further, but they know that something in the colour, design, material is not right, and it's not going to sell at any price, so down it comes. Even in hard times, some women are still choosy.

Having said that people don't seem to do darning any more, the eminent art critic Brian Sewell revealed recently in the *London Evening Standard* that he is a keen stitcher and repairer. He has apparently a dozen pairs of very smart underpants that he dearly loves. Every time a hole appears, he gets out his darning mushroom, needle and cotton, and darns away, repairing the holes.

'Engendered in my childhood,' he wrote, 'habits of economy die hard.'

That's the way to do it.

VITAMINS
for HEALTH

WHOLE MEAL

7 lb

HINDHAUGHS LTD
Gallowgate Mills,
NEWCASTLE-ON-TYNE

HINDHAUGHS
WHOLE ✦ MEAL
RECIPES

5 HEALTH

Governments always want their citizens to stay as fit and healthy as possible, otherwise they will be unnecessary burdens on public services, but in wartime or other times of crisis it is even more important to keep the populace trim and slim, able and active, eager to jump up, fight for the cause, save us from our enemies, real or imagined. In times of belt tightening, metaphorically, it is always good to have people literally reducing their actual belts by a few notches. Don't want stomachs hanging out all over the place.

In my collection of books with funny titles – well, titles I think are quite amusing – one of my favourites is one called *How to be Happy though Married.* I gave it to my wife on a wedding anniversary many years ago. It used to stand on our bedroom shelf, but now I have it my room with my other odd titles.

The book came out in 1889 and the section on health begins with the story of a physician whose books on health sold in thousands – but in fact they only contained four simple rules: 'Keep the head cool; keep the feet warm; take a light supper; rise early.' Still pretty sound advice.

The author is not named, but described as 'A Graduate of

'Hindhaughs Wholemeal Recipes', *c.*1930

the University of Matrimony'. He doesn't appear very much impressed with doctors in looking after us or making us better.

One very popular 1920s book on health was *Every Woman's Doctor Book*. No authors are named, but it was published by the Amalgated Press and sold through various newspapers as special offers or inducements, the sort of medical book my mother had. It must have frightened the life out of many women with its alarmist description of hysteria, which it said could be brought on in young women by unwise diets, late hours and too much excitement. Another big worry was constipation, which affected women doing sedentary jobs, such as typists, seamstresses, machinists. However exercises were recommended which could help.

HYSTERIA

Hysteria is said to occur most commonly in young women, but men and children are also affected. Anything having an unfavourable influence upon the health, such as badly ventilated rooms, unwise diet, late hours, and excitement, encourages the appearance of hysteria. As a rule, some emotional shock, worry, or fright can be traced as the direct cause of an attack of hysteria. . . . A great deal can be done by judicious treatment. Regular occupation which is not too severe is excellent. A lazy, frivolous life fosters an hysterical tendency. In bad cases isolation from sympathetic friends, combined with judicious diet and massage, may be necessary.
Every Woman's Doctor Book, 1920s

Many generations were obsessed by the fear of constipation and worried endlessly about their bowels – and probably led Sigmund Freud to several rather wild theories about anal retention.

I have a friend, Sarah Carrier, whose father was a country GP before the last war and she remembers her mother overhearing an old farmer saying that all the doctor ever gave was two sorts of medicines. 'One for opening and one for closing – and one tastes of cocoa and the other tastes of hoss piss'. By that he meant magnesium trisilicate, to settle the tum and help you go to the

Woman, week ending
23 February 1946

PLATE 3

TO CURE CONSTIPATION (See page 13)

Correct daily exercise is of the greatest importance in the treatment of constipation, because it tones up the abdominal muscles. Here are two excellent exercises. In No. 1, squat as shown in the first photograph, balancing on the toes and with the arms outstretched to the front, palms downwards. Then rise swiftly into the position shown in the second photograph, keeping on the toes and swinging the arms above the head. Repeat three or four times, gradually increasing the number, without causing fatigue.

Here is Exercise No. 2. Lie on the back as shown in the photograph above, the hands clasping the knees, the head slightly off the ground. Then release the knees and push them forward till the soles are on the floor and the body upright; at the same time shoot hands forward, clenching them.

Do these exercises on rising and before going to bed, and persevere with them, for you must not expect immediate results. Wear the loosest possible clothing — pyjamas or a nightdress are best. People with heart disease should not do these exercises without consulting a doctor, and they are best avoided during the periods.

Every Woman's Doctor Book, 1920s

OCCUPATION AND HEALTH

More tiresome than anything else is, perhaps, the harmful effect of a sedentary life, where one has to spend the greater part of the day sitting down. Thousands of machinists, embroideresses, sewing hands, typists, clerks and office workers find that eight out of the nine working hours afford no opportunity for exercise.

Every Woman's Doctor Book, 1920s

loo, and chlorodine with kaolin to bung you up and stop the runs. It was roughly true, but then of course when pencillin came in, he did have proper pills which could cure you.

However, people were always aware that plenty of exercise was about the best way of staying healthy and could be done easily and cheaply as possible – unlike today and the rise of expensive gyms where they charge you a fortune just to lift a few weights or walk on a treadmill, which you could do just as well at home, on your own, and save a great deal of money.

In the 1930s there was a very successful series of books by a Lieutenant J.P. Muller which consisted of fifteen minutes of exercises a day, all of which could be done at home without any equipment or special clothing. The one I have is called *My System for Ladies.* I bought it thinking it was going to be the confessions of a Hollywood gigolo. Lt Muller was in fact Danish – presumably originally some sort of military man – and had secured the patronage of the Prince of Wales, so it boasts on the title page.

MY SYSTEM FOR LADIES

15 Minutes Exercise a Day For Health's Sake

By

LIEUT. J. P. MULLER

The book is full of special exercises for trunk circling, leg swinging, arm circling, body lowering, plus a lot of rubbing of the arms, shoulders, loins and breasts. The illustrations are rather amateur, though not in any way pornographic, perish the thought, and

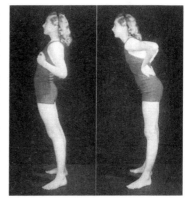

certainly not aimed at readers who later went on to enjoy the illustrations in *Health and Efficiency* magazine. His model for the photographs, all the way through, was his thirteen-year-old grandaughter Mirabelle June, born in 1924. I wonder if she came to regret posing for her grandpa's exercises.

One of the recurring and ongoing elements in physical exercise advice, is that it will not only keep you fit and healthy – but looking rather wonderful, perhaps even beautiful. In *Home Notes* for August 1942, at the height of the war, there was an editorial urging women to keep their figure under control because when peace comes, 'you'll be sorry you neglected your good looks'. The article mentions the BBC's regular series of keep fit exercises, which were broadcast on the radio every morning, doing their bit to keep the nation healthy. There was also the Radio Doctor, giving us good advice on healthy eating.

My System for Ladies, 1930s

During the Second World War one of the points of food rationing was not just to share out our limited resources equally and fairly but to improve health. During the depression years of the 1930s, with 2 million unemployed, reports had shown how unhealthy most people were, especially the poor – some 40 million were deficient in some way, usually lacking calcium. With the outbreak of the war, and rationing, huge efforts were made to improve health generally with such measures as free milk in schools, free orange juice for children and cod liver oil. Endless government leaflets instructed how to have a healthy, balanced diet, stay fit, make the most of ingredients which most people had never seen before, such as dried eggs and dried milk, and explained the need for vitamins, what they were, how to get them.

With less sugar around, less meat and fatty foods but lots of vegetables, there was less dental decay. One good result was that after war people were generally healthier than they had been before. They were less fat, fitter and had been taught to take nutrition and diet seriously.

Manufacturers, of course, when promoting and advertising their products, often appeared to be giving out apparently impartial health advice as if they were working on government orders. Elliman's, who produced a very popular embrocation in the 1920s and 1930s, published a little booklet, priced 6d, which was called *Elliman's Library of Health*. It featured 'Self Massage, for Men and for Women', which obviously was a very cheap way of doing it yourself, without masseurs or

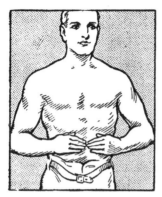

FIG. 37.

SELF-MASSAGE OF THE ABDOMINAL MUSCLES (using Elliman's as a lubricant). Hold the hands as shown in sketch—finger-tips touching. First lean back to contract the abdominal muscles; then massage with the finger-tips with a brisk up and down movement. After this, turn the fingers downwards so that the thumbs come together, and complete by pressure principally from the thumbs in a kneading movement. To relax the muscles for a repetition of the above, simply incline the body slightly forwards.

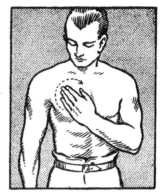

FIG. 39.

SELF-MASSAGE OF THE CHEST (using Elliman's as a lubricant). Stand as shown above and proceed to massage, using a gripping and pinching movement of the fingers throughout. In the case of the right hand on the left breast commence with an *upward* movement towards the left shoulder and continue in a circular direction. *Vice versa* for the left hand on the right breast.

FIG. 38.

SELF-MASSAGE OF THE SIDE OBLIQUE MUSCLES (using Elliman's as a lubricant). Stand as shown and massage thoroughly the whole length of the side muscles with the flat of the curved hand. Repeat this for the right side.

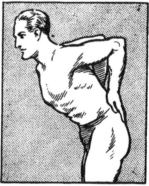

FIG. 40.

SELF-MASSAGE OF THE SMALL OF THE BACK (using Elliman's as a lubricant). This massage is a valuable aid to bodily suppleness. Commence in the position shown, working the hands up and down (pressure always on the *up* strokes). Then hold one hand above the other on the small of the back, exerting pressure on the muscles with the *back* of the hands. In this movement the knuckles may be used freely to exercise the kneading motions of massage. Work the hands simultaneously but in *opposite* directions.

Elliman's Library of Health, 1930s

Rules of Life for Rheumatic People

The following rules of life should be closely followed by all those of a Rheumatic tendency. Prevention is always better than cure, and it is much better to prevent attacks rather than wait for the attack to come on and then apply remedial measures. Repeated attacks can only lead to the further worsening of the general condition, but avoidance of the conditions which foster the attacks is the surest way to keeping free from Rheumatism's scourge.

Always wear flannel next the skin and let the clothing be warm but light.

Have the teeth and throat attended to. Keep the bowels regular.

(These two factors are important, as Constipation, Bad Teeth, and infective areas in the throat are prolific predisposing causes.)

Keep the health good.

Avoid damp, cold, draughts and extreme changes in temperature.

If you have been exposed to any of these conditions have a hot bath immediately, to which a little Elliman's has been added (see Page 9)

and have a good rub down with Elliman's.

Eat plenty of good nourishing food but let it be plain and wholesome. Rich foods are no good to you. Eat brown bread instead of white, and include such fresh vegetables as celery, watercress, etc., in your diet as often as possible. Take alcoholic drinks only in moderation.

Don't let the joints get stiff and set, keep moving them about as much as possible, even though it pains you. Rub them occasionally with Elliman's to preserve suppleness and freedom of movement.

ALWAYS keep this book by you and a bottle of Elliman's in the house, as prompt treatment is the surest way to cut short an attack.

Elliman's Library of Health, 1930s

equipment. It listed eight different exercises to do, from self massaging the 'Side Oblique Muscles' to 'Self Massage of the Deltoids', complete with illustrations, but on close reading of the small print, in each case, it recommended that Elliman's was used as a lubricant.

There was also a feature on the 'Rules of Life for Rheumatic People', which included wearing flannel next to the skin and keeping the bowels regular, plus of course 'a good rub down with Elliman's'.

As today, there were also lots of special diets, or special foods, which were said to contain the perfect ingredients to keep you fit and healthy. *The ABC of Fish Cooking* naturally recommended fish for a young girl slimming or boy who is training.

My Home in July 1938 had a diet which promised to improve women's figure and maintain their vigour – the Bread and Butter Diet. Not something you see recommended today. I suspected it might have been sponsored by the bread manufacturers but it

Keep down your weight but keep up your strength

Have you a girl who is " slimming " or a boy who is " training " ? Give them fish, and they won't worry you any more by not eating proper meals. Fish nourishes without fattening. Because fish is so digestible a good meal of fish can be taken before playing vigorous games. Many famous athletes train on fish.

*The ABC of Fish Cooking, c.*1930

SLIM

while improving your Figure and maintaining your Vigour !

*T*HAT'S the great secret! You have seen how dangerous some slimming systems have proved themselves — how they are followed by loss of vitality and wasting illness.

Be wise and join the NATIONAL SLIMMING CAMPAIGN organised by Elisabeth Ann Loring, the famous diet specialist, in co-operation with a biologist and a distinguished dietitian. Many thousands of women already have improved their figures *and* their general health by this method. Thousands more are adopting it as month follows month. Its success is due to the maintenance of bodily vigour by means of

THE FAMOUS

Bread & Butter Diet

★ But there's more in it than that. *Write for full particulars to:* THE SECRETARY, NATIONAL SLIMMING CAMPAIGN, TRAFALGAR HOUSE, GT. NEWPORT ST., LONDON, W.C.2

SLIM THE BREAD AND BUTTER WAY

seemed to be the work of something called the National Slimming Council. We could do with that today.

The use of organic and whole foods to keep you healthy and fit, though nothing like as extensive as today, goes back many years, with products being promoted as being natural, without all these nasty chemicals, either inside or around them. Before the war, Hindhaughs of Newcastle advertised itself as the producer of the 'original stone ground Wholemeal', and said it was vital for growing children.

My Home, July 1938

PLATE 13

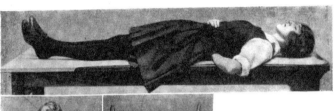

BREATHING EXERCISES

should be performed out of doors or before an open window. Breathe *in* through the nose and *out* through the nose and mouth. The first exercise consists of lying flat on the back and breathing deeply, with one hand on the upper part of the abdomen, which should push against it at each breath, and the other tucked between the back and the table or floor; it should touch *both* throughout the exercise

For the second exercise, first stand as in the left-hand photograph, then raise the arms slowly sideways above the head, breathing *in*, then lower them slowly, breathing *out*. The photograph on the right shows another exercise which is good for developing the chest muscles and remedying flat-chestedness. The exercise consists simply of sitting tailor-wise, lifting the arms above the head, and then, with little jerking movements, forcing them backwards. These exercises are good for anæmia (see page 19) and for children with adenoids. (See page 133.)

*Every Woman's Doctor Book, c.*1930

SEA-SICKNESS

Every year brings with it a new remedy against sea-sickness. Arm yourself with your favourite nostrum by all means – if you are satisfied it is not injurious – but do not neglect the following precautions. Eat a good plain meal two hours before going on board, masticate your food well; and, if possible, take a saline draught in the morning before sailing. Should you after this be attacked by mal-de-mer it will at any rate be much mitigated, and no evil consequences will result. It is not trifling matter to be sea-sick while the stomach is devoid of food and it has often led to a ruptured blood vessel.

Household Hints, 1902

Today, organic foods are everywhere, which to me is usually a euphemism for expensive. I don't fall for such things, but I have to admit that I have succumbed to joining a gym. I pay £45 a month for the privilege of being a member of LA Fitness, which greatly upsets me. I only go there to use the swimming pool as my local council one in Kentish Town in London has been closed for over two years.

But there is one good way to keep fit and healthy, one which has been around for centuries, and is free, can be done at home and does not need any expensive or complicated equipment. In 2008, the Women's Institute produced a series of instruction videos to get us through these tough times which featured, amongst other topics, gardening and home management. It

FOODS FOR FITNESS

AN A.B.C. OF CHOOSING FOODS

'Foods for Fitness', Ministry of Food Leaflet, 1946

also included a sex guide video, which proved highly popular. This gave advice on how to perk up your sex life, the best sexual aids and what positions to use if you have arthritis – which sounded much more fun than having a flannel next to the skin.

The message was that in a time of recession, soaring fuel and transport bills, the high cost of gym membership, the best free, warming, fun and healthy exercise is sexual intercourse. Energetic sexual activity, apparently, can use up all the calories you have consumed in a large slice of chocolate cake. I'm not sure if you should eat the cake before or after sex, but it's not often in the history of health that you get advice on how to stay fit and healthy – and also employ your baking skills.

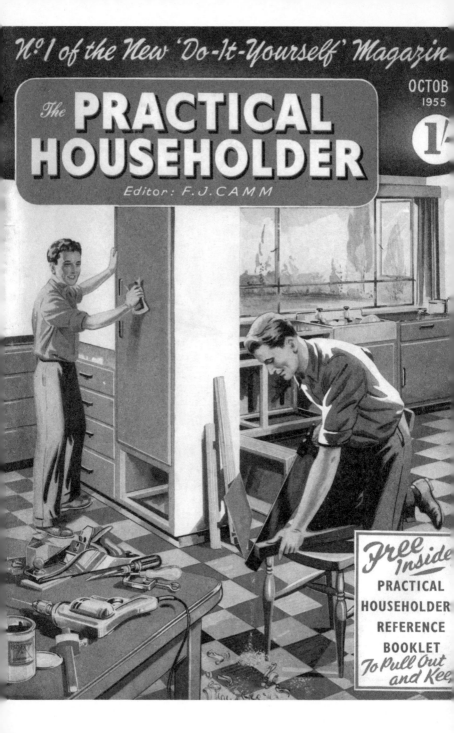

The PRACTICAL HOUSEHOLDER

Editor: F.J.CAMM

OCTOB
1955

1/-

FREE Inside
PRACTICAL
HOUSEHOLDER
REFERENCE
BOOKLET
To Pull Out
and Kee

6 D.I.Y.

My father was rubbish at Do It Yourself, yet when I was about eight, at the end of the war, he got it into his head to make some bookends. I can't remember there being a great need for bookends in our house, as we had so few books, certainly not enough to need a shelf to accommodate them. My mother was a great reader, and went through the whole of Dickens every year, but she got her books from the library. All we had in the house was a medical book, bought with coupons through the *Daily Express*, and a gardening book, via the same source, despite the fact that we didn't have a garden, at least not one that anyone ever looked after.

My father bought a fretwork set, some wood, and some instructions on how to cut out the shape of an elephant, twice of course, to go at either end of his proposed bookshelf.

I can still remember the oaths and shouts as he took over the kitchen, bits of wood and broken fretsaw blades everywhere, with me being ordered to hold tight to the end of the bit he was trying to saw, then blaming me when his hands shook and it all collapsed. I ran out of the kitchen in tears, up the street, vowing never to come home again. In the end, he chucked out all his pathetic, misshapen pieces of wood along with the fretwork tools.

The Practical Householder, October 1955

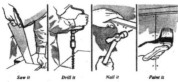

We didn't know at the time that he was in the early stages of multiple sclerosis which soon took over his body, forced him to leave work, confined him to bed, brought about a premature death. I hated him at the time for making me help with his stupid fretwork, but I soon felt sorry, when we all realised he was ill.

It's only now, all these decades later, that I realise that he was behaving like millions of other husbands who had set up home in the 1930s, all whom were being exposed to an avalanche of books, magazines and newspapers instructing, nay, commanding them to Do It Yourself. The message was clear that you weren't a real man,

Homemaker, March 1959

or woman for that matter, for they too were being assaulted by similar images, unless you could knock up shelves, a table, perhaps a garden shed, using little more than a knife and fork and a supply of 4 × 4.

I have copy of *Hobbies Handboook* for 1935, the year before I was born, which is almost 300 pages long and crammed with hundreds of things to make at home and the tools and tricks to make them with. The fretwork section covers pages, full of ads for fretwork sets which start as low as ls-6d and go up to 50 shillings for the state-of-the-art set, which includes a work bench operated by pedals.

Punch, 19 August 1942

ROUTINE **SCRAP** DISPOSAL MADE EASY

WITH A "GREENBAT" BALING PRESS

The systematic baling of scrap is both a national duty and an economy. Waste paper properly baled commands a better price and is much more easily handled. "Greenbat" Baling Presses are made in all types and sizes, from the small hand baler shown above to large-size presses for metal.

GREENWOOD & BATLEY LTD.
LEEDS • ENGLAND

RB B.P.13

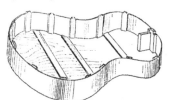

Complete Patterns of this full-size playing instrument which the amateur can make are given on Design Sheet No. 2009, price 4d. The wood, and fittings are provided—complete as set out below.

The interior of the instrument is clearly seen in the illustration at Fig. 1. It is built on a flat back with strengthening pieces glued across, and uprights to take the strain of the sides glued round the edges. The pattern shown is full-size both for the back and front.

The Back

The back is cut in whitewood, but the front (or the top), must be of special pine to produce the musical effect required. A good plan is to cut the upright support pieces with their tenons (C) before cutting the mortises in the top and bottom. Glue the uprights first into the base piece (or back), at the same time temporarily laying on and fitting the top. Do not glue this part yet, however.

Inside the end where the neck joins, there is a stiffening piece of ¾ in. wood which fits in at D, and at rightangles to this for standing along the base, is another stiffener which is shown in the detail at Fig. 2. Across the floor and on the underside of the top are three stiffening pieces. Three similar pieces are glued under the top. The neck itself has six circular holes which are for an ordinary guitar fitting, with pegs. For the Hawaiian style a special machine head with keys is fitted, and for this purpose a slot has to be cut into the neck, as shown by the diagram.

T
HE Hawaiian guitar, as readers will probably know, is an exceptionally popular instrument amongst dance bands, and produces that wailing sound which seems to be an essential of dance music at present.

The opportunity to make it is provided our readers by a special large chart on which the patterns required are set out full size ready to put on the wood. The work can be undertaken with the aid of a fretsaw and a few ordinary carpentry tools.

Complete cutting instructions are given on the sheet as to thickness of wood, etc., and particulars of fittings required are also given herewith.

How to Play

The Hawaiian model is played across the knee and the notes and effects are produced by stopping the strings with a piece of steel. The strumming effect is made by passing the finger across the strings with the steel held in the left hand between the second finger and thumb.

The strings used, unlike most instruments, are of wire, and in order to produce the correct effect, have to be fitted on to a special head, the pegs of which can be turned to pull the strings themselves quite taut.

The principal trouble generally is the shaping of the neck, but to overcome this Hobbies supply one ready for fitting.

Fig. 1—A detail showing how the body is made and stiffened up.

MATERIALS REQUIRED

A special parcel including all wood for body, a neck properly shaped ready for fixing—complete for 7/6. The fittings are a special metal tail-piece with bridge, a set of machine heads and keys, a set of Hawaiian accessories, brass wire for marking notes, and a complete set of strings, 9/6.

The 1s-6d fretwork set, which was probably of the type my father was persuaded to buy, came with '12-inch handframe and saw, steel cutting table, strong 2-inch cramp, six fretsaw blades, a simple design and working instructions'. Could a real chap not be happy with all that? The manufacturer of that particular set boasted that it had been a leading manufacturer of fretwork tools for over thirty years, so the passion for this particular form of Do It Yourself had been going for a long time.

My father was not interested in hobbies, arts and crafts for their own sake, but in making something that would be useful for the house and save him money – and of course help him create something he could be proud of. These were all strong selling points in the marketing of Do It Yourself manuals and equipment.

The range of goods and furniture, objects and machinery which people were clearly making, on their own, at home, by themselves, is astonishing. However did they do it, find the

---

BIRDS, QUADRUPEDS, &c.

To Stuff: Remove the skin carefully, leaving entire the skull, horns, hoofs, tail, etc., of large animals, and the skull and beaks of birds; remove the brains through a cavity made in the mouth: rub the inside of the skin thoroughly with a mixture of alum, pepper and salt, and stretch it out evenly in a cool, airy place. When perfectly dry proceed with the stuffing. For this purpose hay, hemp, oakum, wool, or any suitable substance is used.

Recipes for the Million, 1891

A CHEAP AND PRETTY TABLE ORNAMENT

Take a goblet with the stem broken off, cover it with coarse flannel sewed together to prevent it slipping, stand it in a saucerful of water; wet the flannel and sprinkle over as much flax seed as will adhere to it; replenish the saucer from time to time as the water becomes absorbed by the flannel, and in two or three weeks the flannel will be concealed in a beautiful verdure, which will bear comparison with most table ornaments.

Recipes for the Million, 1891

time and energy, acquire the skills and ingenuity? In that issue of *Hobbies Handbook* there were detailed instructions on how to make your own guitar, electric clock, radio cabinet, standard lamp and even a gramophone. Many of these were must-have gadgets and adornments of the times, which every household longed to have, but they were still very expensive in the shops and beyond the reach of most ordinary working folks.

During wartime, there was an even greater need. People then tried to make some of the necessities of life, such as shoes, not just household adornments or items which were largely decorative. In *The Gadget Magazine* for March 1949 there are some excellent suggestions for making the most of old toothpaste tubes. 'The material with a hundred uses.' The suggestions ranged from cleaning out old tubes and refilling them to contain other more

OLD TOOTH-PASTE TUBES

The foil itself can be adapted for various decorative and other purposes. First slit the tube, open it out flat, and proceed to remove the enamel lettering by briskly rubbing with Acetone and fine steel wool or similar material. This provides a brilliantly polished surface, and any uneven patches can be ironed out by solid rolling with a pencil on a dead even surface. Letters and numerals can be clipped out with scissors, and cemented to glass for attractive signs or house numbers. The best cements to use are fish glue, Shellac, or Copal lacquer to preserve the sheen. Another use for the foil is for decorative designs on wooden bowls, trays of similar utensils. The darker the wood the more attractive is the glistening foil decoration. Other absorbing uses for the foil is to cover ornaments, glass vases, inkwells and a hundred other household articles. Always burnish the complete work with fine steel wool, adding a coat of thin lacquer to protect the surface.

The Gadget Magazine, March 1949

useful liquids and materials to opening them out, bashing them flat, rubbing them down, then cutting them up in pieces, thus providing patches to repair various household objects or for cutting into letters and numbers to stick on your front door. One suggestion was to turn the old tooth paste tube into a soldering gadget. The assumption is that all real men knew exactly what to do with a soldering iron.

The magazine also had hints on how to turn old cans into trays and make a coil spring tag holder, whatever that is, but it promised shopkeepers would find it invaluable in storing price tickets.

A CIGARETTE ECONOMY

Many folks nip off the end of an unfinished cigarette either to reduce their consumption, or – we blush to say it! – short-cut the boss's disapproval. This, at the best of times, is a hazardous procedure, liable to burn the finger tips at least, or cause another Great Fire of London, at most. An easier, cleaner way is to use a snuffer. What is a snuffer? Why, the end of a discarded fountain pen cap, sawn off about an inch from the end. Slip the lighted end of the cigarette into the snuffer and hey presto, it is well and truly out, and ready for re-lighting at the appropriate time without wastage.

The Gadget Magazine, March 1949

A tip marked 'Cigarette Economy' told how to snip off the end of a discarded fountain pen cap and use it as a cigarette snuffer. This would come in handy, so it said, when you wanted to quickly save the end of an unfinished cigarette – and 'we blush to say it' – in order to keep it hidden from the boss that you had been smoking on the job. Tut tut.

In this magazine, and scores of others of the period, there were always instructions for repairing your own lino. Everyone had lino before and after the war – nasty, ugly stuff and hellish cold. I remember in winter time trying to get out of bed in our unheated bedroom, from the bed I shared with my brother, by going straight into my trousers and socks without having to let my bare feet touch the ground. Otherwise you would freeze and be stuck to the lino all day.

In women's magazines, during and after the war, women are seen bending down, repairing lino and carpets and furniture. *Woman* for 26 January 1946 gives instructions on making a useful linen bin stool for your bathroom out of an old tub.

In the first issue of *The Practical Householder* of October 1955, which I have in my collection of Number Ones of magazines and newspapers, there is a mission statement at the beginning, saying what it plans to do to 'answer the problem of rising prices'. It lists a huge range of subjects it will cover, including

The Practical Householder,
October 1955

Our kitchen is transformed !

— and we did it ourselves with

WARERITE *Handy* **PANELS**
Regd.

Making An Electric Gas-lighter

With Details of a Mercury-operated Switch

THE accompanying sketches give details of a mercury-operated electric gaslighter. It is highly satisfactory and does away with the usual manual switching.

The switch is made from a piece of aerial lead-in tube about 1¾in. long and is threaded internally for about ¾in., as in Fig. 1. Next make two brass plugs to fit the tube ends and drill a hole in one and solder a thin brass rod into this plug, as indicated, this rod being long enough to leave a gap of ⅛in. when the plugs are screwed in. To assemble the switch first polish the brass rod and base of top plug so that the mercury will coat them over with a thin film and so make perfect contact.

Shellacing the Threads

Then shellac the threads on the bottom plug and screw in tight, pour in some mercury to the level of the end of the brass rod and screw in the top plug after shellacing.

Handle

Take a suitable handle and bore a hole to suit the diameter of the switch, then at the ferrule end bore another hole to take a length of ⅜in. brass tube and connect the two holes with a central ⅜in. diameter hole, as shown in Fig. 2, to accommodate the connecting flex. Next, solder a wire to each end of the switch, and another to the brass tube as shown, insert the switch and wires and then make an ebonite or wooden plug to fit tightly in the handle with a hole to allow flex leads to pass to battery or, preferably, a bell transformer.

Plugging the Tube

The next step is to make a plug from a

piece of thick, hard fibre, or from several fibre washers, to fit tightly into the open end of the brass tube. Make two brackets A and B (Fig. 3) from strip brass, solder piece B to the side of tube, as in Fig. 2, then pass a bolt with

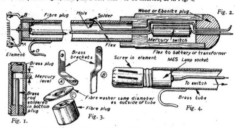

Fig. 1. Sectional view of the completed gas-lighter and details of parts.

wire attached from mercury switch through fibre plug and washer C, through bracket A, and tighten with a nut. Push the plug tightly into the end of the tube. Solder hook D to the tube in the position shown.

Fitting the Element

The element is a piece of resistance wire suspended between brackets A and B with small bolts and nuts. Instead of this type of igniter

a M.E.S. lamp-holder, such as is used for radio pilot lamps, could be soldered in the tube in place of the fibre plug, thus allowing the screw-in type of igniter, which are on sale, to be inserted, as in Fig. 4.

Breaking Contact

When the lighter is hanging handle downwards contact is broken, but the mercury will make contact again before the handle reaches a horizontal position.

The Practical Householder, October 1955

help with laying linoleum, of course, to installing a hot water system. Inside in that first issue there are details on how to make an electric gas lighter, which sounds hellish complicated, judging by the weird diagrams.

Amongst the advertisements is one showing a woman in her pinny standing in their kitchen with her husband who is in his jacket and tie. Both are beaming having jointly totally rebuilt their kitchen. 'Our kitchen transformed! And we did it ourselves.' The seceret, apparently, was Warerite Handy Panels – 'Easy to glue, screw or pin. Easily cut to shape and size. Easy to harmonize.'

Perhaps the biggest project a keen householder could attempt was to build your own house. A booklet from the early 1950s called *Twenty New Bungalow Plans* gave detailed instructions and plans on how to build your own bungalow – at prices from £1,900. Sounds quite a lot to me, when old terrace houses at the time could be had for £500, but having a new bungalow was clarty posh, a true status symbol, and could cost £4,000–£5,000 if you were buying one.

There are people today who still build their homes, often using kits imported from Scandinavia, or yurts made out of old bits of carpet and canvas, or just knock something up out of old wood.

'Twenty New Bungalow Plans', 1950s

roll out the barrel

and make it into a useful linen-bin stool for your bathroom

I n this age of small houses with small rooms we all want furniture that combines minimum size with maximum usefulness. Double-duty pieces are precious—and precious hard to get—but here's one that can be yours for the making; a linen-bin-cum-bathroom-seat.

You make it from one of those small plywood tubs that have contained imported dairy produce or whatnot. You might find one in an oil and colourman's yard, in your grocer's yard or in one of the markets.

Besides the tub you will need some pieces of plywood ½ in. thick; a sheet of compressed cork the same thickness (ordered from your ironmonger); 2 short hinges with screws; ¾-in. panel pins (thin round wire nails with almost no head); paint (undercoating and white gloss or enamel); casein waterproof glue; putty and glasspaper.

Cut down top of tub with a tenon saw to height wanted, remembering that lid and seat will add 1 in. to finished height. The top must be reinforced, to keep its shape and carry the hinge of the lid-seat.

To do this cut with a fretsaw a hoop of plywood 1 in. wide to fit inside top of tub. Slip it in, level with the top; glue and nail in position. You must allow the glue to dry properly —this will take about twenty-four hours.

MAKING THE LID

For the lid cut a circle of ply slightly larger than top of tub; then cut a small section away. Glue and screw this section to the reinforcing ring as shown in the diagram. Fit and screw hinges to the ends of each cut edge, making sure that lid raises and lowers freely.

Now cut a circle from the sheet of cork, using lid as a guide. Trim a section so that it fits front of lid, clearing hinges, and glue it on. Then glue and pin an outer rim of ply, ¾ in. deep, to front of lid, covering the join of cork and wood and paring it away towards the hinges with saw or wood chisel.

Glasspaper all rough edges and surfaces, including cork. Then remove hinges, putty any flaws or ugly joins, and

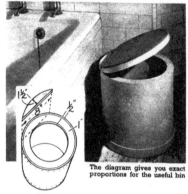

The diagram gives you exact proportions for the useful bin

carry your bin into a spare room or a big, well-lighted cupboard where it can be undisturbed for a few days. Dust it down, shut doors and windows and stand it on a table, with paper beneath to catch any paint drips. Then paint *every inch* of wood, inside and out, with two undercoats and one topcoat. When all paintwork is dry, put back hinges.

There's a reason for this rather tiresome business of taking off and putting back hinges. The bin will be used in a very damp atmosphere where any unprotected wood would warp and rot; therefore all of it, even the wood under the hinges, must be covered with paint to make a sound job. Waterproof glue is recommended for the same reason.

Woman, week ending 26 January 1946

The patron saint of simple living is the American writer Henry Thoreau (1817–62), who built himself a log cabin in the woods and lived there for two years, writing a book about his experiences called *Walden: On Life in the Woods*, published in 1847. He was seen as a bit of an eccentric, and his books didn't do well in his lifetime, but in the last few decades he has become acclaimed as one of the fathers of ecology and self-sufficiency. He recommended intimacy with nature, reduced spending, living off the land, though it came out later that his mom, who lived only two miles away, used to deliver a basket of pies and doughnuts to his log cabin every Saturday.

Today there are communities trying to live an equally simply life out in the woods, but the ordinary householder with ordinary minimal skills, talents and tools would never attempt to build his own house, far less attempt the sort of household improvements, such as that electric gas lighter, which seems to have been commonplace from the 1920s up to the 1950s. The 1950s were of course still a period of austerity, with not much in the shops, not much money in the pockets. After that, well in theory, so we were told at the time, we entered the Age of Affluence. Growing up in the 1940s and 1950s, we never had a car, a fridge or even a phone, far less a telly. Now every working family has all these things, and a lot more beside. When they pack up, or go out of date, we dump them rather than repair them, and buy the latest new version. Manufacturers encourage us to do this, making it

TRAYS from CANS

Convenient—and Cost Nothing !

REALLY handy trys for small mechanical parts, bolts, nuts, screws and nails, can be improvised from empty tins. Split them carefully with a hack-saw, and bend open to the shape illustrated. Several of these trays can be soldered together to form a chain of very useful receptacles for workshop or bench. Lidded tins should have the lids soldered on before splitting. Affix appropriate labels to each tray if considered helpful.

The Gadget Magazine, March 1949

The Practical Householder, October 1955

cheaper to buy new than try and repair old. Hence the art of making or repairing domestic items has long gone.

It's hard to see signs so far in this new age of austerity of any campaigns to encourage householders to Do It Yourself in the mechanical, technical or manufacturing sense. Lots of books on making cheap meals, using cheaper ingredients, how to be thrifty, recycle clothes, the joy of charity shops, how to generally save money, but Do It Yourself seems to have been forgotten, apart of course from the crafts market which is thriving but that is mainly for pleasure not necessity. Perhaps it's too late. Life and society has moved on. We've lost all those skills and desires, preferring – and being able to – buy a new telly pretty cheaply when the old one conks out rather than consulting a D.I.Y. manual on how to make your own flat-screen telly out of match boxes.

However, if things get worse over the next few years, D.I.Y. might come back. Do It Yourself books will start flooding the market, for which you will need shelves. But please, don't try to make elephant bookends. It will only end in tears . . .

Back cover of *Children and What To Do With Them, c.*1881

THE SIGNAL IS **SAVI**

7 MONEY

I have an 1879 copy of Samuel Smiles's classic book *Thrift*. Great book, great title. No messing around. He didn't give it an eye-catching title as India Knight did in 2008 when she published a slim and fairly slight little volume called *The Thrift Book: Live Well and Spend Less*. Other books in the last year or so covering the same theme have included *The Penny Pincher's Book*, *Living for Less* and *Waste Not Want Not*. With Dr Smiles, you got it straight, and at great length: some 150,000 words of sensible, uplifting prose – all of which is as useful today as it ever was. In fact I'm surprised no one has republished it for these hard times.

Samuel Smiles was born in Haddington, Scotland, in 1812, the oldest of eleven children, the son of a shopkeeper. He studied medicine at Edinburgh University and then moved into political journalism, becoming editor of the *Leeds Times*. He then started writing books, beginning with *Self Help*, another simple, self-explanatory title. Pehaps his best known books were his series on the lives of the great engineers, such as George Stephenson, the father of railways, which is a first class piece of work – as long as you skip all the moralising.

'The Signal is Save', National Savings Committee poster, *c.*1940

The New Illustrated, 15 February 1919

Smiles was typical of so many Victorians in that he ascribed to all his heroes the highest virtues, whether they had them or not, using their lives to make moral and religious points.

In *Thrift* there's a lot of that. He tells us that we must practise thrift because it is 'a moral and social, as well as a religious duty' to 'provide against the evil day'. One of the many benefits of thrift is that it 'abates the Curse of Drink'. When he gets going, though, among the sermons and uplifting stories about famous people, there are some good observations about practising thrift and he recommends four rules:

Spend less than you earn.

Pay ready money and never run into debt.

Never anticipate uncertain profits by expending them before they are secured.

Keep a regular account of all that you earn.

Later on he bemoans the desire of people to be seen to be rich, saying that it is worse now than it has ever been. He should have lived a bit longer. 'There never was such a burning desire to be rich. People are no longer satisfied with the earnings of honest industry, but they must aim at suddenly becoming rich – by speculation, by gambling, swindling or cheating.' Or becoming a banker, as it's known today.

He particularly has a go at women for their extravagant ways. 'There never was such a rage for dress and finery amongst English women as there is now.' He feels sorry for the shopkeepers who fall victim to their greed – agreeing to six months' or even a year's credit on the latest fashions, and ending up not getting paid when their husbands find out.

Even the poor are criticised for extravagance, especially when it comes to funerals. He says that an ordinary tradesman will expect £50 spent on his funeral while the funeral of an ordinary labourer usually costs £5-10s, which has naturally led to the massive growth in funeral clubs, with people spending money they can scarcely afford just to have a decent send off. He tells of poor people joining two to three funeral clubs and quotes one instance of a man in Manchester who had insured himself with nineteen funeral clubs.

Funeral clubs were a massive business throughout the nineteenth century and the first half of the twentieth. I can remember my own grandparents still saving a penny a week for their own funerals to avoid the disgrace of having a pauper's death without a decent burial.

One of the most pernicious forms of was funeral club was for babies. There was a sliding scale whereby you could insure against a child dying before the age of five, which cost only a few pennies a week, but all you got back was £3 when they died. Or you could insure them up to the age of ten and get more money back, but of course you paid for more. It was an age when all classes had large families – and lost many of them long before they grew up.

Dr Smiles did, however, approve of people saving their money in building societies, run-on co-op lines, with all members being shareholders, which of course was the original plan, still the practice with some today, though many in recent years turned themselves into banks, and went on a wild spree with our money. Smiles mentions by name the Leeds Permanent and the Burnley Building Society, names we still recognise.

Many other writers and pundits, apart from Smiles, gave readers the benefit of their advice on how to be prudent and save money. And also how not to be conned. The *Englishwoman's Domestic Magazine*, which was edited by Mrs Beeton's husband, gave a warning in 1863 about innocent country girls falling for a series of alluring advertisements. For a sum of two guineas, they were promised lessons in lithography, which would enable young women to make loads of easy money. 'A most unremuneratve investment,' so they sternly warned.

A new magazine called *Money Maker*, which first appeared in November 1899, gave a list of hints for living wisely, which are mostly very similar to Smiles' – such as pay ready

EASY INCOMES

We believe that many evil disposed people, principally inhabiting London, lay cleverly-baited traps, and gins, and snares for the entrapping of unsuspecting persons. The traps they set are in the form, sometimes, of advertisements, cunningly concocted, and inserted in the newspapers. These advertisements are various in diction, shape, garb, and extent, but they all tell nearly the same tale, which is this: that by the expenditure of a small sum of money, payable by installments from time to time, some secret will be imparted, some trade furnished, some art taught, by which the possessor or learner will be ever after able to have much profit.

The Englishwoman's Domestic Magazine, 1863

money, keep accounts, avoid waste. It advises keeping an eye on servants, encourage them to be thrifty. It also warns that cheap things are not always the best bargains, and can turn out uneconomical, a warning that still appears every week in one domestic magazine or other.

This new magazine, like many others, was in the business of telling you how to make money as well as save it, with alluring adverts for earning easy money by sitting at home making sweets or clothes, which you sent off to a central point, or how you could become instantly rich by correctly answering competitions and puzzles and win big money prizes. The magazine had one excellent tip for making money out of cigar ends which was apparently practised in Paris on a large scale and basically

Answers, 25 April 1891

consisted of picking up old cigar butts, opening them up, then selling the tobacco.

A rival magazine called *Fortune*, in its 25 October 1904 edition, describes some clever ways to keep your money and treasures safe at home without the use of banks, such as putting cash in the family Bible, under the mattress, in the pockets of an old dress, or in old shoes. Jewellery, it suggests, can be kept in a coal scuttle as burglars won't think of looking there, which sounds precarious to me.

That edition of *Fortune* promised 10,000 prizes for readers, the biggest of which was based roughly on lucky numbers, printed in each copy, which had to be collected over four issues. The prizes, for 1904, were pretty stupendous, starting with a new Humber two-cylinder motorcar. Second prize was a horse-drawn carriage – a Lady's Park Phaeton. Other prizes were a billiards table, a drawing room suite, a typewriter. It's an interesting insight into what were considered the must-have status symbols in 1904.

It was *Tit-Bits*, which first appeared in 1881, that led the way in offering enormous prizes to readers who entered their com-

OLD-FASHIONED SAVINGS BANKS

The pocket of an old dress that hangs in an unconcealed way in a closet is regarded by many women as one of the safest places imaginable for spare rings, brooches, and bracelets, and even for a pocket-book. Old shoes, standing in their proper place beside new ones, are likewise much esteemed, for a great deal can be put down in their toes without giving the slightest evidence of value therein. Money and jewellery reposing among the coals in the coal-scuttle commends itself to many owners on leaving home for a brief period.

Fortune, 25 October 1904

"TIT-BITS" SYSTEM OF LIFE INSURANCE.

ELEVEN CLAIMS HAVE BEEN PAID.

ONE HUNDRED POUNDS will be paid by the Proprietor of "Tit-Bits" to the person whom he may decide to be the next-of-kin of anyone who is killed in a Railway Accident in the United Kingdom, provided a copy of the current issue of "Tit-Bits" is found upon the Deceased at the time of the catastrophe. This offer does not apply to Railway Servants on Duty. No payment made in case of Suicide.

Tit-Bits, 28 January 1888

petitions In November 1883, the first prize was a London house. The other innovation credited to *Tit-Bits* was an automatic insurance policy, which you were given purely by purchasing a copy of the magazine. It meant your next of kin got paid £100 if you were killed in a railway accident, and had on your person a copy of *Tit-Bits* ('No payment made in case of suicide'). By 1891, it was claiming it had paid out to thirty-six relatives of dead people. It's a sales gimmick which so far modern newspapers, in their struggle for circulation, have not got round to copying.

Being thrifty, saving money, avoiding too much extravagance, is obviously sensible to do at any time, but in times of war it became vital. Ordinary people had to take care of their own money and curb their expenditure, but if they had any spare cash, the government was keen to get their hands on it, telling us how necessary it was if we wanted to win the war to invest in various forms of government war bonds and savings accounts. In Salisbury during the first war special leaflets were dropped by aeroplane, encouraging local people to buy war bonds so that they could be turned into aeroplanes. In London, the whole

First World War War Bonds leaflet, dropped by aeroplane

Mock battlefield set up in Trafalgar Square to publicise War Bonds

In December 1944, the Ministry of Information informed the nation that there were now 298,000 Savings Groups, who had managed to raise £8,467 million to help the government's war effort – an average of £177 per head of the population. Out of every £100 received by the average British citizen, £19 was saved and £36 paid in taxes, leaving £45 for 'living'.

of Trafalgar Square was turned into a war zone – to advertise buying War Bonds to 'Feed the Guns'.

The origins of government savings schemes go back to 1873 and the Savings Bank Act, but it was the First World War that saw the first savings certificates being issued and the National Savings Movement being established on a large and national scale. The government was desperate for money to fight the war, promising of course that our savings would be 100 per cent secure with them. Volunteers in work places and schools, and local savings committees, organised collections.

The same thing happened in the Second World War. I can remember as a child taking 2s-6d to school every Monday, goodness knows where my mother got it from, and would be given a stamp which got stuck into my savings book. When you got to eight stamps, you got called out and presented with a certificate, feeling very important, affluent and of course terribly patriotic.

'War Savings', 1942.

VOL.3. No.9

WAR SAVINGS

FIGHT
WORK

BLUE PRINT
FOR VICTORY

SAVE

"She Sells Savings Stamps" in a
B.S.A. factory in the Midlands.

West Cumberland News, 21 April 1941

SOME LETTERS FROM OUR READERS

I am sending you a photograph of some young members of our staff, most of whom are under 17. They made sales trays for savings stamps and decorated them with suitable posters and slogans, such as 'Savings Stamps won't break you – but they will break Hitler.' In two months they had increased sales by 1,700 per cent.

A.W. Foster & Co. Ltd., Bardney, Lincs
'War Savings', 1942

When my own children were young, I started Savings Certificates in their names, which they were very grateful for when they got to eighteen, and were able to go off on a gap year and waste it all. But it did serve one purpose. I had told them in advance that they had these savings coming when they got

10/- and it's yours!

Each 10/- Certificate becomes 13/- in ten years — an increase of 30% free of tax. And you can hold up to 1,000 of these new Certificates *in addition* to any you already hold of previous issues.

Issued by the National Savings Committee

Radio Times, 6 June 1947

to eighteen but on one condition. They were not to start smoking. Otherwise that was it, no savings.

The Post Office savings bank, backed by the government in the form of the Postmaster General, was another form of National Savings. Like National Savings, it brought people into the world of finance, savings and investments who would otherwise, at least up to the 1960s, have had no knowledge or experience of stocks and shares or even owning their own house.

I'd always thought the notion of buy to let was a modern concept, brought in by cheap mortgages in the 1990s and the theory that property prices would go up for ever and ever, so

UNBEATABLE !

A
£395 SEASIDE HOME
AT SALTDEAN, THE SEASIDE SUBURB OF BRIGHTON, THE QUEEN OF SEASIDE RESORTS.

IT CAN BE MADE TO PAY FOR ITSELF
£5 INITIAL PAYMENT SECURES £5

Saltdean possesses a splendid beach. The finest Open Air Coloured Swimming Pool on the South Coast. A Sun bathing Sand Lido with Restaurant and Tea Gardens. A Children's Paddling Pool and Boating Lake. A Wonderful Promenade, Undercliff Walk and Great Marine Drive. A Magnificent Hotel, to accommodate 600 guests, will be completed this year and is expected to be ready about July 1st.

[See over

Good Housekeeping, April 1938

that whatever happened, just by doing nothing, you were sitting on a capital improvement every year. So I was surprised to see a glossy advert in a copy of *Good Housekeeping* for April 1938 that was specifically aimed at those thinking of buying a holiday home to let on the south coast. It featured a detached house at Salt-dean at the 'unbeatable!' price of £395. By letting it out for only two months a year, so it claimed, it could be made to pay for itself.

The arrival of Premium Bonds brought

During special 'Warships Weeks' between October 1941 and March 1942, over £545 million was raised in government savings – enough to cover the cost of building five battleships, four aircraft carriers, forty-five cruisers, 300 destroyers, thirty-three submarines, 267 mine sweepers, 160 corvets and 117 depot ships.

in a new element to the government's methods of getting us to save money with them – by introducing the chance of randomly winning money. They were introduced in April 1957 by Harold Macmillan and £5 millions worth were sold on the first day. The attraction was that your money was safe, but you also had the chance of winning a £1000 prize, if Ernie was kind to you – ERNIE standing for Electronic Random Number Indicator Equipment. Over £100 million was taken in the first full year. Today about £10 billion goes into Premium Bonds each year, and there are now two prizes each month of £1m. So they say. I have yet to hear of anyone admitting to being a million-pound winner.

The Premium Bonds are clearly a huge success, encouraging us all to save, plus the chance of a little flutter and big lottery win, but somehow I don't think good old Dr Smiles would have approved of them.

Built to Save you money

...this new big family "12"
costs less to buy and less to run

—yet is built to high Vauxhall Standards

THIS big family "12" is new and opportune. It embodies every proved Vauxhall quality feature and provides an answer to the present-day problem of cutting expenses without sacrificing convenience and enjoyment.

The Vauxhall 12-four will save you money on every mile and give you better, smoother, safer and livelier 12 h.p. motoring than has been possible hitherto.

We welcome comparisons, hope you will take the wheel on *all* cars of similar power and even higher price and—let a ride decide.

Vauxhall dealers everywhere are ready to provide full facilities for an adequate trial.

PRICE
This Vauxhall 12 h.p. four cylinder car (Tax £9) costing from £17 to £50 less than other British twelves, offers unprecedented value. It maintains the Vauxhall's usual high standard.

PETROL SAVING
Despite outstanding performance, petrol economy is unique. Under normal driving conditions 35 m.p.g. is assured.

SMOOTHNESS
Trouble-free torsion bar independent suspension — proved best of all types — turns riding into gliding and makes *all* roads smooth. The special engine mountings make the already smooth engine still smoother.

SAFETY
All-steel integral body construction gives greater strength with less weight; simplifies and cheapens repairs.

PERFORMANCE
In spite of roominess of the saloon, in spite of petrol economy, the performance is quite outstanding and we welcome a comparison with any other "12".

ROOMINESS
A really comfortable family car; attractive in appearance and tastefully upholstered. Plenty of luggage space.

THE NEW
VAUXHALL
12 four

Write for new magazine style catalogue, it will interest you.
Vauxhall Motors Ltd., Luton, Beds.

STANDARD SALOON £189 · DE LUXE SALOON £198

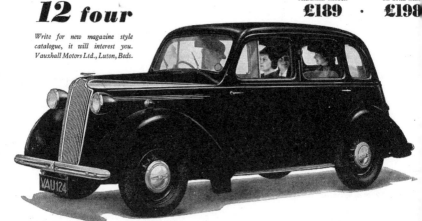

8 TRANSPORT

In tough times, in poor times, people go back to bikes as the cheapest, easiest form of transport, apart of course from walking. Cycling relies on your own power, not that supplied by an outside and usually wasteful and expensive force. It's always been popular, for lots of obvious reasons, since it was first invented, but it's noticeable that governments don't do much to support cycling until they get in a panic, usually caused by the latest economic crisis or fuel shortages. They then desperately try to encourage us to get on our bikes, thereby hoping to decrease traffic congestion, save fuel, and make us happy and healthier.

A German called Baron von Drais in 1817 is usually credited with creating the first bicycle – i.e. something with two wheels – but his was made of wood which you pushed along and jumped on when you got up a bit of speed. It wasn't until the end of the century, in the 1890s – by which time chains, brakes and pneumatic tires had come in – that cycling mania swept Europe, the USA and then the whole world.

Women particularly took to this new craze, finding freedom and an independence they had never experienced before. They

The Illustrated London News, 10 September 1938

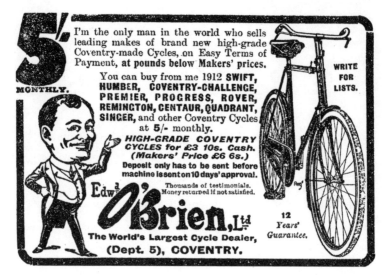

I'm the only man in the world who sells leading makes of brand new high-grade Coventry-made Cycles, on Easy Terms of Payment, **at pounds below Makers' prices.**

You can buy from me 1912 **SWIFT, HUMBER, COVENTRY-CHALLENGE, PREMIER, PROGRESS, ROVER, REMINGTON, CENTAUR, QUADRANT, SINGER,** and other Coventry Cycles at **5/- monthly.**

HIGH-GRADE COVENTRY CYCLES for £3 10s. Cash. (Makers' Price £6 6s.) Deposit only has to be sent before machine is sent on 10 days' approval.

Thousands of testimonials. Money returned if not satisfied.

Edwd O'**Brien,**L^td

The World's Largest Cycle Dealer, (Dept. 5), COVENTRY.

Years' Guarantee.

12 Years'

5/- MONTHLY.

WRITE FOR LISTS.

Answers, 8 June 1912

wore long skirts to hide their legs and discarded their restricting corsets. Bloomers came in and new fashions arrived, but it was freedom of movement, the ability to go anywhere safely and unchaperoned, which was the biggest benefit. 'Cycling has done more for emancipation than anything else in the world,' wrote the American writer Susan B. Anthony in 1896.

Mass manufacturing brought the prices down and they were soon within the reach of almost everyone. Once you'd made the original outlay, they were fairly cheap to run. Cheapness and economy was always stressed in the advertisements, especially those aimed at young people. Bikes lasted a long time, if they were cared for properly. A large advert in *Chums* magazine for February 1908 offers to repair and totally rejuvenate your old bike for the new season for only 35 shillings. As we know,

HAVE THAT BIKE READY

The merry cycling days are fast approaching, and if you intend to use your last season's machine again, **NOW** is the time to have it rejuvenated. Perhaps you intend selling it; if so we can double its selling value for the outlay of a few shillings, for instance—We will strip your machine in every detail, true-up the wheels, cones, &c., add entirely new ball bearings throughout, thoroughly enamel in best style the entire frame, forks, wheels and mudguards, heavily plate the handle-bars, brakes, seat pillar, cranks, pedals, chain-wheel, and fork crown; re-assemble and adjust it, all for **35/-** And you, as a cyclist, know that that means making it

A NEW CYCLE FOR 35s.

We will thoroughly overhaul your machine, true-up the wheels and cones, add new ball bearings, adjust and re-assemble it for	We will enamel in best possible style your pair of rusty wheels for	We will enamel in best style the entire frame and forks for
10/-	**3/6**	**5/9.**

Your Machine converted into a Two-speed for 25/-!

| We will fit to your machine a genuine Villiers Two-speed Hub for **25/-**; but only while present stock lasts. | Or a Sturmey-Archer Three-speed Hub ... **45/-**
B.S.A., or Armstrong Three-speed Hub ... **45/-**
The New All-speed Gear **50/-**
Eadie Two-speed Coaster **47/6**
Three-speed Coaster ... ... **52/6** | We will fit to your cycle a genuine Eadie Two-speed Hub (⅛th inch pitch) for **35/-**; or build same into an entirely new wheel for **40/-** |

Any part of machine or fitting built, or any idea carried out to customers' wishes. Let us have your enquiries; our extensive department for this class of work will prove economical to you.

Now we have told you what we can do for you in the way of transforming that old bike of last year into "a thing of beauty and a joy for ever," up to date in its splendour of new enamel, bright nickel and variable gears, with its sweet, easy-running new bearings, we want you for your own sake, as well as for ours, to see to it **NOW**, and not wait until the rush comes.

Estimates free for carrying out repairs and renovations to your own ideas.
Remember—our prices are reasonable.
We do not put any work in hand until you have approved of the prices we send you.
The department is the finest equipped of its kind in this country, and stands for both efficiency and economy.
Think it over; let us know what you have decided to have done, but see to it **NOW**.

A. W. GAMAGE, LTD., HOLBORN, LONDON, E.C.

Chums, 19 February 1908

studying the history of belt tightening, recycling comes in cycles, but was this the first evidence of recycling cycles?

My father-in-law rode the same bike for over fifty years, going to work on it to his metal box factory every day. Despite lots of clever improvements in designs and materials, gears and gadgets, bikes still look roughly today as they did 100 years ago.

In 1950, my biggest, most passionate desire in my whole life was to own a green Raleigh Lenton Sports with Sturmey Archer gears. Oh, how I dreamed of having one. I would go everywhere on it, be happy for ever, if only I had the money to buy one. It came to pass when I took on two jobs, before and after school, delivering papers and groceries, which enabled me to pay 13s–11d a week to T.P. Bell in Abbey Street, Carlisle's

> **The Ministry of Information reported in 1942 that the production of all motor cars had been suspended, along with refrigerators,pianos, lawnmowers and vacuum cleaners. Only 540,000 bikes were manufacturerd that year, compared with 1,600,000 in 1935. The ordinary person who could not show urgent necessity for using a car was not allowed any petrol.There were no excursions or special holiday trains running in the whole of the UK.**

best known bike shop. I half thought this fantasy was peculiar to me, that I had dreamed it up on my own. Many years later, when I met John Lennon, I found that he had owned the very same bike at around the very same time. I hadn't realised that all boys of that age, all over the country, had been dreaming the same dream.

We never had a car, not in our house, though they came in around the same time as bikes became popular, around the 1900s. Motoring was seen as either a sport or a status symbol at first, so expense and economy were not important considerations. Then when motorcar factories were introduced, conveyor belts turning them out in millions, prices dropped and they were soon in reach of the working man, or at least the upper reaches of the white-collar working classes. In the USA, the Ford Model T first appeared in 1908. The big revolution in the UK was the arrival of the Austin Seven in 1922, which sold for £167 – still a lot for most workers.

The 'Comfy Cars' open charabanc, Paignton, Devon, early twentieth century

Those who couldn't afford their own motorcar could always have a spin in a giant luxury charabanc model while enjoying an annual holiday, on the Isle of Man or the South Coast. Passengers would have their photograph taken, looking suitably affluent and pleased with themselves, which could be turned into postcards then sent home to all their friends.

In my lifetime, the big breakthrough in motor transport, for cheapness and economy, was the creation of the Mini by Alec Issigonis in 1959. I bought my first in 1960, or it could have been early 1961, but I know the price was £500. The colour was blue, which led to a big argument with my wife about it, as I maintained it was grey. It was then I that realised I was colour blind.

'Wizardry on Wheels', 1959

When I took it home to Carlisle for the first time, and gave the old folks a whirl round the countryside, people came out of their houses to look at it. It was the square shape and smallness that was so unusual, just 10 feet long, yet it could hold four people.

A few years later, while working as a journalist on the *Sunday Times*, I happened to interview Aldous Huxley, visiting from the USA. I offered him a lift back to his hotel in my Mini. He had great trouble getting in, as he was about 6 feet 6 inches, and then in Piccadilly he tried to get out, while I was still driving. A London double-decker bus had come alongside and its wheels towered over us, frightening the life out of him, convincing him we were about to be crushed.

The cheapest form of transport, apart from bikes, was the railway, which revolutionised so many aspects of life – allowing suburbs to be built, fresh vegetables and newspapers to be delivered almost anywhere, offering cheap transport and cheap holidays to everyone, either to the seaside, Lake District or even abroad to Paris. Thomas Cook first started his holidays by running cheap day trips by train. In 1841 he took 570 temperance campaigners the 11 miles from Leicester to Loughborough, charging them one shilling for the rail fare and food. So began package holidays.

Cheap train travel had a big influence on the rise of football, the nation's most popular pastime – players could travel further for away games, and so could supporters. It was traditional when a northern team came to London for the Cup Final, even from the furthest north-west or north-east, that railway companies would lay on cheap day returns. Then when they got to London, the 'Metro' offered the most direct and cheapest way to Wembley itself.

All forms of paid-for transport get hit in times of recession as people are forced to cut back on expenditure generally. In the Great Depression in 1929–32, a quarter of the workforce in Scotland and the North was out of work. When the Jarrow workers wanted to protest, they didn't take the train or their bikes, but marched to London on their own two feet.

'Travel by "Metro" to the Cup Final', Metropolitan Railway poster, 1923

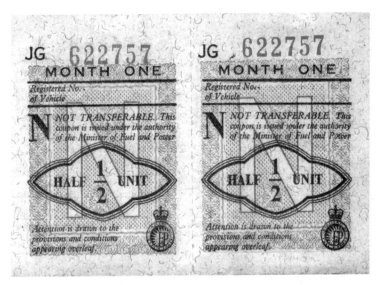

Second World War motor fuel ration book

During the wars, the problem was different. It wasn't just a matter of lack of work and money, but lack of fuel. Measures then had to be implemented to control the use of fuel, which meant rationing. There was no petrol rationing during the First World War – cars were not as prevalent and rationing anyway came in late.

In the Second World War, petrol rationing started as early as September 1939, and continued until May 1950. There were special petrol ration books and coupons, and also different coupons if you were running a motorbike.

The populace was encouraged not just to conserve fuel but to take as few journeys as possible – thus, so it was argued, we would have a better chance of beating those nasty Nazis. Advertisements told us 'Don't Make Unnecessary Journeys'.

A WAR
OF *MOVEMENT*

MODERN warfare depends on Railways as never before; they are of supreme strategic importance. British Railways are fighting and winning the greatest "War of Movement" in the world's history. Remember this and DON'T MAKE UNNECESSARY JOURNEYS.

RAILWAY EXECUTIVE COMMITTEE

Punch, 15 September 1915

Manufacturers did their bit by bringing out products which, so they claimed, would save fuel consumption if you added a few drops of their patent liquid – at least that's what this 1943 advert for something called Scrubbs, cloudy ammonia, appears to promise. It's not clear how it worked. Presumably it helped to remove grease and dirt without using soap, which was in short supply, rather putting in your petrol tank.

During the Suez Crisis of 1956, the Ministry of Fuel and Power, worried by panic buying and hording of petrol, brought in petrol rationing once again. Farmers, essential council works and, perhaps surprisingly, ministers of religion, were allowed more petrol than the rest of the population, while doctors and medical workers could get as much as they needed.

In 1974, when the miners' strike led to the three-day working week, electricity and

Punch, 22 September 1943

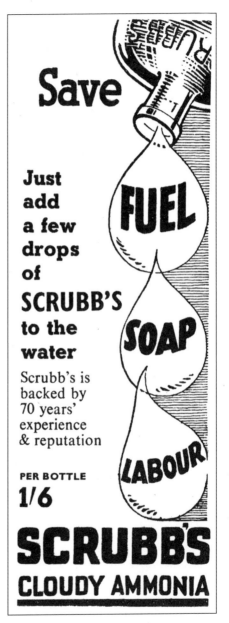

Save

Just add a few drops of SCRUBB'S to the water

Scrubb's is backed by 70 years' experience & reputation

PER BOTTLE 1/6

FUEL

SOAP

LABOUR

SCRUBB'S CLOUDY AMMONIA

gas were rationed – in the sense that they were cut off for certain hours every week and people had to eat cold suppers and go to bed by candlelight to keep warm. I bought a paraffin heater, which gave off a nasty smell, and used that on cold nights when there was no gas or electricity. I still have it, covered with dust in the garage, ready for the next fuel emergency.

There was soaring inflation and high oil prices, which had contributed to the government being so tough on the miners, but they never actually got round this time to rationing petrol. Petrol coupons were printed and issued by the Board of Trade and Industry, but never used. I've still got mine – ready for the next round of belt tightening.

I'm surprised that petrol rationing did not come in 2008, especially when the price of oil went sky high and petrol at the pumps jumped to £1.24 per litre before it came down again. But there was an extensive campaign to make people use cars which consumed less fuel, making it more expensive to drive big, gas-guzzling monsters by increasing taxes on certain vehicles. Drivers were also advised to drive slowly and so get more miles to the gallon.

One new innovation in recent years, to decrease the cost of motoring, has been the introduction of car pools, whereby you join a car club, pay an annual fee, which enables you to pick up a car at certain points and then leave it, without having to own it or tax it. Sharing rides has also been tried, with special lanes devoted to cars containing more than one

Don't make any mistake—
remember

"YOU GET SO MUCH
MORE IN AN AUSTIN"

£250

THERE MUST be a reason why you see such a big and increasing number of Austins on the road. There is. Every day more motorists are proving that it takes a car of the Austin standard of quality and dependability to give the "intensive service" modern motoring conditions demand.

● GOODWOOD FOURTEEN SALOON *WITH THE NEW ENGINE £350*
DE LUXE SALOON WITH PYTCHLEY SLIDING ROOF £260 *(prices at works)*
Have you seen the Austin Magazine for May!
B R I T I S H   C A R S — B E S T   I N   T H E   L O N G   R U N

Country Life, 7 May 1938

person. In the old days, hitchhiking was very popular, and you always managed to get a lift, but this has now come to an end as people have become scared of strangers.

The other day, while waiting near Gospel Oak station, I saw a large London Transport poster showing two petrol pumps. Above one were the words 'Pump of Costliness' with the pump showing lots of £££££ signs. The other pump had the words 'Pump of Happiness'. Below it was a pair of training shoes showing a smiley face. The main message was: 'Why Not Walk?'

It was all a bit complicated, and it seemed strange for London Transport to be advocating walking, but I suppose they were only doing their bit in these hard times, sending out the same sort of messages we had during the war with regard to transport. Is your journey really necessary?

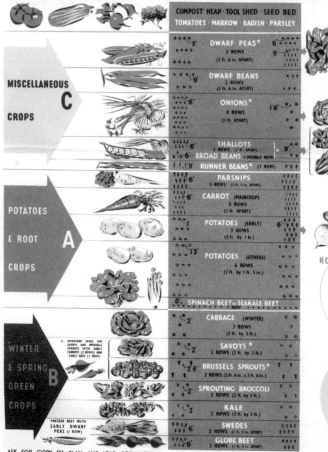

DIG FOR VICTORY

Grow for Winter as well as Summer

THIS PLAN WILL GIVE YOU YOUR OWN VEGETABLES ALL THE YEAR ROUND

COMPOST HEAP · TOOL SHED · SEED BED
TOMATOES · MARROW · RADISH · PARSLEY

MISCELLANEOUS C CROPS

DWARF PEAS* 3 ROWS (2 ft. 6 in. APART)	**INTERCROP WITH SPINACH (2 ROWS) AND FOLLOW WITH LEEKS 1 ft. APART (4 ROWS)**
DWARF BEANS 2 ROWS (2 ft. 6 in. APART)	
ONIONS* 8 ROWS (1 ft. APART)	**FOLLOW WITH SPRING CABBAGE (4 ROWS 1 ft. APART)**
SHALLOTS 2 ROWS (1 ft. APART)	**FOLLOW WITH WINTER LETTUCE**
BROAD BEANS 1 DOUBLE ROW	**INTERCROP WITH SUMMER LETTUCE**
RUNNER BEANS* (1 ROW)	

POTATOES & ROOT CROPS A

PARSNIPS 3 ROWS (1 ft. 3 in. APART)
CARROT (MAINCROP) 5 ROWS (1 ft. APART)
POTATOES (EARLY) 3 ROWS (2 ft. by 1 ft.)
POTATOES (OTHERS) 6 ROWS (2 ft. by 1 ft. 3 in.)
SPINACH BEET or SEAKALE BEET 1 ROW

FOLLOW WITH TURNIPS (1 ft. APART)

WINTER & SPRING GREEN CROPS B

*INTERCROP SPACE FOR SAVOYS AND BRUSSELS SPROUTS WITH EARLY CARROTS (2 ROWS) AND EARLY BEET (1 ROW)

CABBAGE (WINTER) 3 ROWS (2 ft. by 2 ft.)
SAVOYS* 2 ROWS (2 ft. by 2 ft.)
BRUSSELS SPROUTS* 2 ROWS (2 ft. 6 in. x 2 ft. 6 in.)
SPROUTING BROCCOLI 2 ROWS (2 ft. by 2 ft.)
KALE 2 ROWS (2 ft. by 2 ft.)
SWEDES 2 ROWS (1 ft. 3 in. APART)
GLOBE BEET 2 ROWS (1 ft. 3 in. APART)

PRECEDE BEET WITH EARLY DWARF PEAS (1 ROW)

ROTATION OF CROPS

1ST. YEAR	2ND. YEAR	3RD. YEAR
C	B	A
A	C	B
B	A	C

ALLOTMENT OR GARDEN

PLOT ...... 90' x 30'

APPROX. 10 SQ. RODS POLES OR PERCHES

ASK FOR COPY OF PLAN AND 'DIG FOR VICTORY' LEAFLET No. 1 or write for free copies to Ministry of Agriculture, 55 Whitehall, London, S.W.1.

9 GROW YOUR OWN

The word 'allotment' means a share, a dividing up of some asset, and in terms of land, the use of the word goes back to Saxon times when land was held in common with the locals each having their share or strip on which to farm. The Normans rather ruined this idealistic system, allowing lords to take over common land, which is why today in the British countryside so much of the land is still owned by the aristocracy.

Today, the word 'allotment' normally refers to urban use, to those little patches of hidden-away scraps of apparently leftover land where traditionally old men escaped to their sheds to watch their onions grow and their pigeons fly.

As with so many aspects of our modern lives, urban allotments as we know them today go back to Victorian times when the poor, especially those in tenement blocks, were encouraged to grow a few vegetable on patches of nearby land provided for them by the local authority in order to keep them out of mischief, i.e. the pub. There was an Allotments and Cottage Gardens Act in 1887, which established the principle, but not all local authorities could be bothered to do much about it.

'Grow for Winter as well as Summer' Dig for Victory leaflet 1, *c.*1940

It was the First World War that increased the demand for allotments and the need for more home-grown produce. One of the most active participants in the campaign to increase allotments use were the railway companies who allowed and encouraged their employees to grow stuff on spare bits of land beside the railway tracks, land which was not suitable for proper agriculture, and which they didn't want the public at large to go roaming over. This is the reason you still see today so many allotments clinging to the sides of railway embankments.

During the Second World War, the need to grow more at home was even more important once the German submarines starting sinking our supply ships bringing food to Britain. This time there was a massive and concentrated campaign, spearheaded by Churchill himself. 'Every endeavour must be made to . . . produce the greatest volume of food of which this fertile island is capable.' The campaign had a snappy slogan 'Dig For Victory', which neatly hinted at how patriotic you would be, growing your own. By 1943, the number of allotments had reached a record 1,400,000 which meant almost every household in the land had someone in their family digging away.

Apart from allotments, people were encouraged to dig up their lawns in their back gardens and grown vegetables, keep chickens, rabbits, goats and even pigs. Public spaces and public parks had flowerbeds and rose gardens removed as more space was required for growing vegetables and fruit. I remember when we first moved to London in 1960, to a flat in the Vale

TO EVERYONE WHO HAS OR CAN GET AN ALLOTMENT OR GARDEN

Owing to the shipping position we shall need every
bit of food we can possibly grow at home.
Last summer many gardens had a surplus of
perishable vegetables such as lettuce and cabbage.
This winter those same gardens are getting short
not only of keeping vegetables such as onions,
carrots and other root crops, but also of fresh winter
vegetables such as later cabbage, savoys and kale.
We must try to prevent that happening this year.
Next winter is going to be a critical period.
This leaflet tells you how to crop your ground to
the best advantage so as to get vegetables all the
year round.
Please study it carefully and carry out the
advice it contains.

R. S. Hudson

Minister of Agriculture & Fisheries
'Grow for Winter as well as Summer'
Dig for Victory leaflet 1, *c.*1940

of Health in the middle of Hampstead Heath, being told that during each war, the Heath had had sheep grazing on it. I didn't believe it, until I saw a postcard.

The Ministry of Agriculture gave out leaflets and instructions telling you how to grow crops in your allotments, such as potatoes, parsnips, tomatoes, marrows, radishes, peas, onions, carrots, cabbages, kale, and how to rotate the crops so

On Parliament Hill, Highgate

Postcard showing sheep on Hampstead Heath, 1916

something was coming up almost all the year round. It also advised how to rotate them over a three-year cycle, to get the best out of the land.

Well-known artists and graphic designers were hired to make attractive 'Dig For Victory' leaflets and posters, some of which today are collector's items and often get shown in exhibitions and displays.

The popularity of allotments continued after the war and an Allotments Act of 1950 directed that local councils should make sure that 4 acres of allotments were provided for every 1,000 of the population. But after the austerities of the 1950s, and the general increase in affluence which began at the end of the 1960s (or so we were told at the time), allotment use declined and by the 1970s they had dwindled to around 500,000. Greedy or short-sighted councils started selling off disused or underused allotments for developments, and by the 1990s they were down to 300,000.

DIG FOR VICTORY   LEAFLET No. 14

Drying ⋆ Salting ⋆ Pickles ⋆ Chutneys

DRYING

CERTAIN fruits and vegetables can be dried in the home quite simply and without expensive apparatus.

The fruits that dry best are apples, grapes, pears and stone fruits, but some varieties, especially of plums, are more suitable than others. Soft fruits and berries are not generally satisfactory.

Leafy and root vegetables are best used in the fresh state whenever possible. Peas, beans and, of course, herbs, may be dried, but most other vegetables are best dealt with by storing them in the ways set out in " Dig for Victory Leaflet " No. 3, or preserving them by other means.

are covered with muslin to prevent the fruit from sticking.

Temperatures

Great heat is harmful : scorching must be avoided. When an oven is used, the door should be kept ajar, and the temperature should never exceed 150°F. Drying can well be done with the heat that remains in the oven after cooking is finished, drying being continued on several days if necessary.

A plate-rack over the fire can often be used, but care must be taken to ensure that smoke does not pass through it. A drying cupboard is also suitable, but the process will probably take longer.

'Drying, Salting, Pickles Chutneys' Dig For Victory Leaflet 14, *c.*1940

'Simple Vegetable Cooking', Royal Horticultural Society, 1940

The decline has now stopped, and everywhere there are long waiting lists for allotments. They are quite cheap, if you can get one, or are willing to wait a few years until your name comes up – as low as £10 a year in some areas, up to £100 in others. The traditional old feller with his scraggy string of tired onions has been replaced by whole families, usually of a middle class persuasion, growing their own basil and radicchio or young single women and men digging for victory over those nasty supermarkets or the scurge of GM foods. Trying to be self-sufficient does bring a glow to the face and gleam of virtue to the soul.

Getting back to the land, communing with nature, growing your own, has become a fashionable activity these last few years, with an increase in magazines, books and television series devoted to the subject, but the present economic problems have made it even more attractive as a way of saving money, saving waste and of course saving the planet.

One interesting effect of our sudden realisation that waste was, er, such a waste occurred at the end of 2008 when the European Commission abolished several dozen of their more dopey rules that had stipulated that our veg and fruit should conform to a certain shape and size. It meant that edible produce previously considered too ugly, too big, too small or too misshapen could now be sold in our shops and supermarkets – and of course was great news for tabloid newspapers and cheap TV shows who had enjoyed themselves so much finding parsnips shaped like breasts and carrots which looked like penises.

The main reason for the change was the fact that it was realised that 20 per cent of fruit and veg produced by farmers was being chucked away, just because of its looks. 'In the current climate of the credit crunch,' said a Sainsbury's spokesman, 'we cannot continue to waste this much food before

In 1943, the Ministry of Information reported that since the war had begun, 7 million acres of grassland had been ploughed up and the area of arable land in the UK had increased by 43 per cent. Half the wheat used for flour was now home produced. Imports of all food had been reduced by 50 per cent since the beginning of the war.

it even leaves the farm.' A EU spokesman said: 'This marks a new dawn for the curvy cucumber and the knobbly carrot.'

While people are going back to digging their own patch and producing their own, they don't on the whole seem to go for the sturdy, boring old-fashioned stuff such as potatoes, parsnips and onions. They prefer to go for exotic herbs, unusual vegetables or even attempting stuff that traditionally no one ever tried to grow in wartime allotments, such as figs, olive and wine-making grapes, but then global warming is supposed to be soon turning us into a Mediterranean country.

One of the countryside activities that is very popular in towns is now beekeeping. It's estimated that £165 million a year is generated by the bee industry. One group of enthusiasts, the North London Beekeepers Association, has a waiting list of sixty who want to join. One problem is a disease, first identified in England in 1992, which threatens to ruin the whole of beekeeping. Will the government step in, provide funding, research and information, artistic leaflets and posters, just as they did in the 1940s when they wanted us to grow more parsnips? They might do.

I haven't as yet seen many pigs reappear in urban back gardens, or goats, or rabbits reared to be eaten rather than cuddled, but it could happen if conditions get worse. Hens are becoming more common and I have seen a sudden increase in recipes for squirrels. I haven't come across much evidence of them being eaten during the war, judging by the contemporary records I have been reading, so in one respect we could be ahead of our 1940s grandparents.

> ## SEASONABLE WORK
> **In most districts of the British Isles, the season when bees are able to store surplus honey is very short, being unually of less than two months in duration. Everything, therefore, should be made ready to assist the bees, in different, or even bad weather.**
> *Farm Life*, 27 May 1905

Grey squirrels in the Lake District and Scotland are considered a pest, as they are endangering the survival of our native and much prettier red squirrels. I often hear the cry from my friends in Loweswater when they kill another grey: 'Shoot a Grey – Save a Red'.

In London, grey squirrels have also become a curse, having increased in number and become bigger and bolder. So it would make sense to try to catch some of the little buggers, especially the ones digging up my bulbs. And then eat them. As you throw them in the frying pan, you can shout 'Eat a Grey – Save a Red'. After all, for centuries we have eaten wild rabbit, so the arts of catching and skinning them can't quite have been lost. As squirrels normally feed on nuts, they should be quite healthy and nutritious, though the urban variety, the cheeky ones taking over the London back gardens, have been spotted in dustbins, picking out cigarette stubs. Let's hope they were just recycling, taking them home for their nests – Do squirrels have nests? – rather than for their own consumption. Best therefore to stick to country squirrels. There was a recipe last week in our local *Camden New Journal* for 'squirrel jambalaya', which sounds quite delicious.

For those not quite up to growing your own, or willing to dig up the back lawn, or kill and skin your own squirrels, rooks and magpies, you can always help out by encouraging people who are growing their own, doing their bit, and, of course, doing it organically and cleanly. The increase in farmers' markets, all over the country, has seen more and more people, not just traditional farmers, running their own smallholdings, growing and then selling their own produce.

One has recently opened near me, in the playground of a local school, and naturally all the right-on families, in their green wellies and Barbours, rushed up Kentish Town High Road as if they were about to climb Scafell, scrambling excitedly to buy all the lovely natural, home grown produce.

I was amazed to discover that this market was part of the London Farmers' Markets, which began in 1999, and now, after ten years, has sixteen different markets run all the year round every weekend all over London. Each week

HORTICULTURAL ENTHUSIAST (WHO HAS JUST BOUGHT A COTTAGE, TO HIS GARDENER): "WE'LL DO GREAT THINGS TOGETHER, PERGOLAS, SUNDIALS, HERBACEOUS BORDERS, STONE WALKS, AND—ANYTHING ELSE YOU CAN SUGGEST?"
GARDENER: "CABBAGES DOES VERY WELL 'ERE."

The Humorist, 14 July 1923

30,000 people attend them and the annual turnover is £6.5 million. There are very strict conditions if you want to get a stall in these markets. You must have produced the stuff you are selling yourself and all of it must have been produced within 100 miles of London. This meant that someone who wanted to sell grouse was not allowed nor another person offering organic olive oil, which of course can't quite yet be successfully produced in the Home Counties.

Grow your own is doing well again in these hard times, but eating stuff produced by other people who are growing their own, that's certainly a growth industry.

10 HANDY HINTS

I've never personally felt I needed any hints about reducing waste or saving money, as I have gone through life never knowingly and certainly not willingly thowing anything out.

I usually say it's down to be being brought up in the war. We were urged to save everything – save waste, money, fuel, energy and that way we would win the war, so there was a good reason for it. The modern-day recycling campaigns that have been introduced all over the country, with local councils supplying special bins and containers for each sort of waste, are no more than what happened during the war. In fact the posters and leaflets and slogans are very much the same, telling us to save wastepaper, old metals, old books, old clothes, bones, broken glass, and put them out in different containers or the appropriate recycling centre. Only the artwork is different.

However, I suspect I would be as I am anyway, despite what I told my children. I've always been thrifty and hated waste. My wife too was brought up during the war, and from exactly the same place and similar background, yet she has never been a hoarder of any type. Her first reaction to almost everything is 'chuck it out'.

If I go shopping, I am given a list which says at the top in

Home Notes, 15 August 1942

heavy capitals 'NO BARGAINS'. She studiously avoids 'three-for-two' and should she get to the checkout counter and a kind assistant points out that what she has is on special offer and that she can get another one, exactly the same, for free, she always says firmly if rather primly 'no thanks'.

She would never think of going to car boot sales, charity shops or even street markets, yet I am devoted to all these places. She is not a spendthrift, or extravagant, which I have to add quickly, or I'll be for it. She is always prepared to make do, spin out what she has in the house, or do without. It's just that when she's buying something, if it's what she set out to acquire, what she was after, then she instantly gets it without regard to the price. She doesn't see the point of trailing round all the shops and stalls, comparing prices, looking for bargains, or buying more than you need just because it's free or cheap. Research has shown that people today do waste about a third of the food they buy, usually part of some three-for-two bargain, which ends up rotting in the fridge and has to be thrown out.

Rotting fruit is a challenge to me. I test all the apples or pears or plums in a bowl first and always pick the soggiest, oldest, mouldiest to eat. I feel good, saving waste, saving money, while my wife and all our children will go 'ugh' and refuse to touch anything remotely off, always going for the best in show.

I've always turned off lights, shouted at them to close doors and keep the heat in. I don't think I've had any brand new clothes for years, except Christmas presents: usually shirts or pullovers, bought by my family. If forced to buy a new pair of shoes, I trail around for bargain shoes, usually made of plastic which I wear till they fall to pieces. At present, I have only one pair of shoes which I wear in the winter months along with my free airline socks. I collect several pairs every January when we go on our annual foreign holiday to the West Indies (which proves I might be thrifty, but I can still spend money, oh yes). In the summer, I live in plastic sandals – in fact Birkenstock, which are not cheap – and bare feet.

I always have my bath after my wife has had her bath, using the same water. Now this is something I picked up in the war, or I like to think I did, though I was a bit young to remember George VI on the wireless telling us about his bathroom economies and how he got into the same bath with the Queen and they only used six inches of water. I could have got some of the details wrong, but the principle is the same. I feel really good using my wife's bathwater – it saves not just money but time and energy by not having to run my own hot water.

SOUR MILK

Never throw it away. For mixing cakes it is preferable to fresh milk, and produces a much shorter and lighter cake. It must not be mixed with fresh milk. If very sour and thick, beat it up with a little water, and strain off any lumps.
Household Hints, October 1902

I am always picking up and keeping odd bits of strings, old wrapping paper, plastic bags, used envelopes and those elastic bands discarded on the pavements and doorsteps by modern postmen. 'Don't they know there's a war on?' I hear myself muttering.

I'm not sure what I'm going to do with all this stuff I've collected but I can't bare to see any of it being wasted.

Luckily, in reading through hundreds of handy hints which have been trotted out over the last 100 years, I did find a suggestion on what to do with odd bits of string. You buy a large pair of knitting needles – and knit the bits of string into a dishcloth. Brilliant tip, huh?

KITCHEN ECONOMY

Save all pieces of string that come round parcels of all kinds, knot them together, and wind in a ball. Get a pair of No. 9 steel needles, cast on 40 stitches, and knit plain a piece twelve or fifteen inches square. These make excellent dishcloths, and the knots help to get the burnt marks off pudding-dishes, etc.
The Best Way Book, 1914

OLD HINTS

Here's a selection, in no particular order or arrangement, of some handy hints, advice and guidance and tips that have appeared over the last hundred years or so from government departments, experts, manufacturers, magazines, books and writers.

The tests on how to detect dodgy food go back to 1935 and a booklet called 'Information: Hints and Ideas'. I haven't tested them, so don't blame me if they don't work, or indeed any other hints in this book. It's social history, innit. But some of them could be useful or informative today.

Picture Post, 6 December 1952

Tests for Food

Defects and how to trace them

IT is common knowledge that many modern food products are adulterated, and it is therefore necessary that all housewives should be in a position to test the goods supplied to them. The following are simple but effective tests for the various articles concerned.

Sugar.—Burn a little in an iron ladle. Pure sugar will burn quite away. Impure sugar will leave some ash behind it.

Milk.—An easy test for milk, failing the regulation glass tube supplied by the public analyst, is to put a bright steel knitting-needle into the milk; if, on withdrawing it, the milk adheres and drops off slowly, it is pure; if, on the contrary, it runs off quickly, leaving the needle bright, it has been adulterated with water.

Tea.—Drop a piece into the fire, and the bluer it blazes the better the tea.

A Ham.—Stick a sharp, clean knife into the ham, under the bone. If it comes out clean, and the smell is pleasant, it is all right. But if there is a disagreeable smell and the knife is smeared, reject it.

Tinned Fruit.—When using tinned fruit, always plunge into the contents of the tin a bright steel knife. Let it remain a few moments, and if there be the smallest degree of copper present it will be found on the blade.

Olive Oil.—Olive oil is so valuable an item in the kitchen that it is well to know which is the best to purchase. A deep brownish-yellow or dark-green oil should be avoided. The very best quality is a light green, while oil that is almost colourless, or that shading to a golden yellow, may be used safely.

Butter.—When butter is heated, it bubbles and burns. Margarine boils cheerfully, and has a distinct odour.

Coffee.—When purchasing ground coffee gather a little in the palm of the hand and press it firmly. If it sticks together in a ball, or cakes in lumps, it contains some adulterating substance. Pure coffee falls apart when the hand is opened.

Pickles.—Chop up a little of the suspected pickle, mix together equal quantities of ammonia and water and pour over it at once. Fasten down securely, and in a short time the liquid will become blue if there is any copper whatever present.

Tinned Meat.—A sure method of testing all tinned foods is to press the bottom of the tin with the thumb. If it makes a noise like a machine oil can when it is pressed, the tin is not airtight, and the contents, therefore, are unfit for use.

Mussels.—When boiling mussels, put a small onion with them. If there is any poison in the mussels the onion will go black. If good, the onion will retain its natural colour and will not taint the mussels in any way.

Mushrooms. — When cooking mushrooms, for safety's sake place a sixpence in the vessel in which they are cooked. If the silver shows the least discoloration the mushrooms are unfit for use and should be thrown away.

Information, Hints & Ideas, autumn 1935

Good Housekeeping, April 1938

ROUGH HANDS

The housewife would never get rough hands if she kept a box of ordinary powdered starch on the sink. Every time she puts her hands in water she should dry them, drip them in starch, and rub for a minute.

LEMON JUICE FOR FRECKLES

An anti-freckle lotion can be made by mixing together equal parts of glycerine and lemon juice, and adding a pinch of borax. This should be dabbed on the skin with a piece of cotton wool.

The Best Way Book, 1914

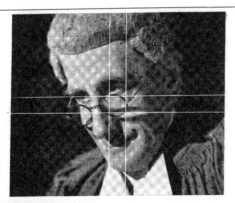

Guilty or not guilty?

Do you smoke every pipeful right down to the last shred and knock out only dust and ashes ? Or do you sometimes throw away a dottle of unsmoked tobacco ? Then read these hints on

'How to make your tobacco last longer'

1 Keep your tobacco in good condition. If it gets too dry, put a small piece of damp blotting paper in pouch or tin.

2 Fill from the bottom of your pouch. Pack evenly and firmly but not tightly enough to stop an easy draw.

3 An occasional *outward* draught through the pipe keeps it alight, if it shows signs of going out.

4 A small piece of clean paper (a cigarette paper for choice), crumpled into a loose ball and put into the bottom of the bowl before filling, will prevent waste, and stop bits of tobacco entering the stem.

FOUR SQUARE

Punch, 16 September 1942

SAVING FATS

Fats are essential for health and strength. It is our duty
to see that not a scrap of fat is wasted in our homes.
Do we always scrape thoroughly the papers in which
butter and margarine have been wrapped? The papers
themselves should be saved for greasing baking dishes or
covering food while it is cooking in the oven.

Wise Housekeeping in Wartime

Woman,
week ending
29 December
1945

MEAT

There are many ways of cutting up the remains of cold meat, and the manner in which this should be done depends entirely upon the nature of the dish to be made. Do not cut the meat into even slices, rather divide it into fancy shapes such as cutlets or fingers; it is thus more easily disguised, and the dish will be much more pleasing in appearance.

Mrs Beeton's All About Cookery, 1920s

YORKSHIRE COUNTY SALVAGE DRIVE: SEPT 6TH TO 20TH 1941

Mrs Smith is helping to win the war!

Every Yorkshire housewife can help to win the War by putting out for the Salvage Collector ALL Old Books, Magazines and Paper, ALL Old Metal Ornaments, Tools, Door Knockers, Etc., ALL Bones and ALL Rags—they're all needed for vital munitions and supplies. AND, all scraps of Food are wanted, too, to feed the Pigs and Poultry.

AND NOW, MAKE *Every* WEEK A SALVAGE WEEK!

Issued by the
LEEDS SALVAGE DEPARTMENT

Leeds Salvage Department leaflet, 1941

Turning off lamps – and radio sets, too – when you leave a room should be a matter of habit. Two hours' waste of your radio every day uses up half a hundredweight of coal a year at the power station.

'Fuel Sense Saves Money in the Home', leaflet issued by the Ministry of Fuel and Power, *c.*1940

SAVE MONEY AND VITAL WAR MATERIALS

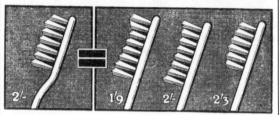

1 WISDOM *equals* **3 ORDINARY BRUSHES**

A WISDOM Toothbrush costs only 2/- (including 4d. tax) yet lasts three times as long as an ordinary toothbrush. Thus by buying a Wisdom, not only do you save money but help conserve vital war materials. The plastics used in toothbrush handles are wanted by the R.A.F. It is real saving, national and personal, to buy a WISDOM.

Wisdom REGD.
TOOTHBRUSH

Punch,
12 May 1943

SECOND-HAND FURNITURE

Well-kept, clean second-hand furniture may often be bought for less price than common new articles. Care should be taken in the selection. It is not advisable to purchase second-hand bedding, carpets &c., as infection and vermin are sometimes carried by them. Mahogany tables, bookcases, chests of drawers &c., in good condition, may be chosen without much danger; but they should be examined to see if dry rot has set in.

Domestic Economy, 1896

MODERN HINTS

In 2008–9, the papers were filled with awfully clever and wise suggestions about how to survive in these hard times. Women columnists who just a few months previously had been telling readers how to track down that must-have £499 handbag or a £995 pair of Jimmy Choo shoes were now advising on making presents out of cardboard and shopping at charity shops.

The middle classes who dumped all their unwanted clothes and kitchenware on charity shops in the good times have stopped donating and are returning to pick up bargains. Save The Children, which has 120 shops across the UK, is running out of stocks and is appealing for more donations.
Independent, 12 October 2008

The new euphemism for charity clothes is 'gently used', according to Lady Sarah Apsley who runs a second hand garment website. 'People realise that gently used clothes aren't a badge of shame – they're a badge of honour.'
London Evening Standard, 4 November 2008

Use leftovers for pack lunches, advocates a campaign group called Love Food, Hate Waste. They claimed that people spent an average of £3.33 a day on their lunch, which was the same cost each day of the food they threw out. Sales of lunch boxes were soaring, but it was best to pack them by looking in the fridge first, then concoct a lunch out of all the leftovers.
November 2008

Save a fortune on expensive face creams and exfoliator creams, which cost around £40, and instead, suggests India Knight in her book *The Thrift Book: Live Well and Spend Less*. 'Get six plain uncoated aspirin – price, pence. Crush them with the back of a spoon. Mix with water to make a paste. Put the paste on your face. Leave for ten minutes. Rinse off, massaging as you go. Pat face dry. Open eyes. Look! Your skin looks about a million times better. Use once a week, twice in emergencies.'

Miss Knight also suggests saving on expensive dry-cleaning bills by buying the Hagerty Dry Cleaning Kit, price £8.99 from Lakeland. 'Cleans about 16 items. Use without fear – it's brilliant and works, even on big things such as coats, for 56p a pop.'

Another handy guide, *The Penny Pincher's Book Revisited* (2007) by John and Irma Mustoe, gave hundreds of good tips which included: Never go grocery shopping when you are hungry; refrigerate candles and they will burn more slowly; pour olive oil into a pepper shaker to sprinkle, not glug; freeze new tights overnight before wearing.

Waste Not Want Not (2008) published by L&K Designs, lists 200 ideas for recycling and reusing everyday things in a modern way. Use old egg boxes to store Christmas tree baubles or golf balls. Cut the flaps off old cardboard boxes and use them as dust protectors for laptops. Milk or juice cartons can make excellent bird feeders by cutting an entrance hole and sticking in a few twigs for birds to perch on. Old newspapers rolled up, with one end cut into strips and feathered, and the other end tied with an old elastic band (at last, a use for my rubber bands) can be used, wait for it, to remove cobwebs. Plastic bottles are easily turned into cloches for the garden by cutting the tops off. Old tights, when filled with potpourri and secured with ribbon and tied to your rear view mirror, make an excellent air freshener for your car. And before you go on holiday, don't forget to place some clingfilm over your computer keyboard to keep out the dust.

When the going gets tough, the tough get down on their knees. More than a quarter of people in a recent poll said they had tried praying, and 42 per cent of them reported a 'positive effect'.
Guardian, 15 November 2008

The Church of England put a 'prayer for the current financial situation' on the prayer page of its website and saw traffic increase by one third.
Sunday Times, 12 October 2008

If praying doesn't work, then poaching could be worth a try. Under the headline 'The Return of the Poacher', the *Independent* reported that 'as times get harder in Britain's cities, armed gangs are heading for the countryside – and stealing deer, salmon and rabbits to feed a burgeoning black market in food'.
Independent, 17 November 2008

The artist Gavin Turk's latest work *Mappa del Mundo*, on show in London in November 2008, was created from detritus he had collected from the streets – crisp packets, drinks cans, cigarette packets, which he then squashed and rendered into a two-dimensional map of the world.

Domestic items created from other discarded objects were going on sale. Blacksmith Dan Harding made a line of free standing multi-fuel stoves out of old parts from Volkswagen cars. They were not cheap: £2,250 for each stove. But they were a limited edition.

In the winter of 2008–9, John Lewis reported that the sale of hot water bottles had increased by 24 per cent.

Meanwhile, sales of bottles of water, so popular in the previous ten years, suddenly started to collapse when people realised that tap water was cheaper and tasted much the same.

Dentists were doing well, after an upswing in people coming for treatment as a result of grinding their teeth caused by worries about money and the economic crisis.

So did hypnotists. Monica Black, a hypnotherapist from North London, who specialised in City workers, reported an increase in business. 'A lot of people in the financial sector are so stressed and nervous about their performance and their jobs being on the line that my clients have more than doubled.'

Car insurance claims were down – as drivers drove less often and more safely.

At Christmas 2008, Argos reported a 300 per cent increase in sales of their £399 fold-up bikes.

Two eco-design students from Goldsmiths College, Sarah Lucy Smith and Rose Clearly-Southwood, have started a company which manufactures environmentally sound underwear. Their first knickers were 'our global warming knickers, made with heat reactive ink and organic cotton,' says Sarah. 'When warmed up, you see an image of the sea overcoming the land.' Other underwear, for men and women, under the Green Knickers banner, are produced using a mixture of bamboo, hemp, silk or reclaimed and recycled fabrics ranging from old curtains to duvets.

All right-thinking literary folks must have been appalled by a so-called 'Helpful Hint' for making your own frugal Christmas presents which appeared in the *Guardian* on 13 December 2008. It suggested a way, with instructions and a diagram, of creating a unique clutch bag. You take one hardback book – and then cut out all the pages, gluing on fabric and webbing to turn it into a handbag. What sacrilege. Now that is taking Make Do and Mend too far.

On 5 January 2009, Boris Johnson, Mayor of London, wrote in the *Evening Standard* that we have to 'recognze that this downturn is a big, brute fact and that we must therefore learn recessionomics'. What's that, Boris? 'By that I mean how to make the facts of the recession fit our agenda for London.' So that was reassuring. Next day, the *Daily Mail* announced with a great fanfare that it was going to SAVE YOU MONEY and launch a 'brilliant new daily guide to all the best credit crunch bargains, cheap deals and money-saving tips'. Day 1 was devoted to – cheap phone calls.

WAR ECONOMY:—
WHERE'S DADDY'S BEST COAT?
I WANT TO MAKE A KETTLE HOLDER!

12 HUMOUR IN HARD TIMES

One of the things that has struck me, looking back over a hundred years or so of advice on how to belt tighten, has been how often the invective, and many of the hints, have been repeated in much the same way every time we have had some sort of crisis, for whatever reason. We have to avoid waste, spin out the pennies, save resources, make do as much as we can with what we have, do it ourselves if possible and at all times be prudent.

The big difference is that back in the nineteenth century, many of the pundits, such as Dr Smiles, and national institutions, were motivated by moral and religious reasons. They did believe it was a sin to be an extravagant wastrel, which would naturally lead to even worse sins, such as drinking and ungodliness.

This theme continued for many years. I have a Maidstone and District bus ticket for 1914 which on the back has the words: 'Waste Paper is Invaluable. Wasted Paper is Wicked.' The idea of wickedness related to waste has all but gone, though of course during the Second World War wasting food was illegal and people were sent to prison. But no one now thinks they'll go to hell if

'War Economy', postcard by Lucie Mabel Attwell, First World War

" WHY, MISS ANGELA, I DIDN'T KNOW YOU RODE A BICYCLE."
" AS A MATTER OF FACT, I DON'T, DEAR. I ONLY WHEEL IT. BUT IT MAKES ONE
FEEL SO MUCH MORE ' COMME IL FAUT,' DON'T YOU THINK ? "

The Humorist, 9 March 1929

they don't collect together all their old newspapers and put them out in the right bin on the right day. In some areas, though, local councils have been threatening to punish you, if not with prison or hellfire, with stiff fines, should you break the rules.

In these godless times, threatening hell and brimstone, moral purgatory, going to the devil, would not carry much weight. But we do have gods today – and they tend to be green. Green gods, such as Sustainability, Biodiversity, Carbon Neutrality, are the ones people worship. Worshippers and true believers now do things to save the planet rather than save themselves from hell.

People are saving and being careful anyway, in this period of economic uncertainty, and it clearly makes sense for everyone to conserve what they have without having to consider any moral overtones, but this element of environmental righteousness as opposed to religious righteousness is definitely an extra incentive for many people to do their bit. What are you doing for recycling, people ask each other, when once they might have asked 'What are you doing for God?'

'They Can't Ration Love', postcard, 1918

Fortunately, before we get too carried away, searching for hidden meanings and patterns where perhaps none exist, another element has been running through all these different periods of constraint – humour.

There have always been those looking to take the piss out of our elders and betters, rulers and experts, authorities and governments, when they have been telling us how to behave, how to save, how to make do and mend. Cartoonists usually managed to find something funny even in wartime, during rationing and with all the po-faced instructions on how to turn old curtains into a new ball gown or make something clever out of cardboard.

During the First World War, Lucie Mabel Attwell (1879–

THIS MEMBER IS HEREBY

FREE $^{OF}_{ALL}$ INSURANCE

ALL - IN ($^{RUN\ OR}_{NOT}$) POLICY $^{ONE\ THIRD\ THE}_{ODDS\ FOR\ A\ PLACE}$

This Non-Tariff Incomprehensive All-In Policy covers all risks ; covers everything but life, death, accident, burglary, disease, fire, third-party, riots, act of God, deluge, and anything that happens during war-time or peace. Also note that

YOU ARE NOT INSURED AGAINST

penal servitude, baggy eyes or trousers, querimoniousness, palsy, winkle-poisoning, floating kidneys, nail biting, hobnail liver, mumps, jactitation and divorce costs, dustification of the uvula, back-fires, punctures, quiddling, callosities, premature execution, baldness, I.O.U. writers' cramp, miner's thirst, after damp, blight, bigamy, xerostomia, quench-lessness, bibativeness, matrimony, Eton crops, staggers, somniloquence, giggling, gumboils, scurf, dandruff, cauliflower ear, rotten bridge hands, blushing, scorpions, hold-ups, hi-jacking, vertiginousness, hornswogg-ling, borborygmus, vermin, synthetic blondes, knock-outs, second childhood, bad eggs for breakfast, troglodytism, foot-and-mouth disease, wash-outs, zelotypia, whooping cough, turf losses, income tax frauds ; also

We do not Insure BITSERS.

BITSER TIN   ⎫ nailed together ⎰ MAKE A
BITSER BOARD ⎭   ⎱ FORD.

Free Insurance Treble.

We Insure—

    Your DOG against RABIES
      ,, COOK ,, BABIES
      ,, SELF ,, SCABIES

For further particulars see Christmas Number of " Our Pets."

Insurance Certificate issued by Ye Ancient Order of Froth Blowers, 1930s

In early 2009, as the economic crisis continued, the jokes going round – some of them a bit sick – were mainly at the expense of bankers, who were being blamed for everything.
'How do you get a banker out of a tree?' Cut the rope.
'What's the difference between a banker and a pigeon?" A pigeon can still put a deposit on a Ferrari.
'What's the capital of Iceland ?' About £2.99 at close of trading.

1964) did many humorous if rather twee postcards, usually featuring children, which were sent to the troops to cheer them up. But she did manage at least one card raising a smile out of war economy.

Insurance companies usually made a good living during times of stress, encouraging the population to insure against anything from death to redundancy, but they were nicely mocked in a little booklet produced by a drinking club founded in 1924 who

'Just to let you know we've patched it up again', postcard, 1910

called themselves Ye Ancient Order of Froth Blowers. Members who joined the club were given free insurance, but it did not cover insurance against baggy eyes or trousers, baldness, Eton crops, bad eggs for breakfast, foot and mouth disease, turf losses, though it did cover your dog against rabies and your cook against babies. All very studentish, a bit like *Private Eye* in their parodies.

Private Eye itself, in 2008 and 2009, ran several joke pieces mocking all the sometimes pretty banal instructions then appearing in many newspapers on how to beat the credit crunch. Their suggestions to try to stop feeling gloomy and cheer yourself up included :

Sit in the garden and watch the leaves turn yellow.

Talk to yourself. It's nice to have someone to listen to you!

Have a good scratch. Doesn't that feel good?

To save money, their hints included:

Save on hot water by taking your washing into the bath and doing it there.

Turn your spare bedroom into an indoor allotment. And if it's big enough, why not keep chickens or a goat? Remember the average spare room can feed a family of 15 for a year.

Save pounds by not buying newspapers full of drivel like this.

Punch cartoon 19 October 1942, mocking 'Dig for Victory' when playing fields were being used for vegetables.

In 2008, a whole book appeared, written by an online satirist going by the name of Ethan Greenhart, mocking some of our current obsessions: *Can I Recycle My Granny?*

I think my favourite comic postcard on the subject of small businesses feeling the crunch appeared during the depression of the 1930s, done by the famous Donald McGill (1875–1962) who was normally better known for his saucy seaside postcards. On the back of my copy, it says the card is being given out with the compliments of M. Hilton and Sons, Wholesale Fish Merchants in Grimsby.

The cartoon shows some sort of shopkeeper or small businessman, listing all the things he's had to suffer, and saying that the only reason he has stayed in business is to see **WHAT THE HELL IS GOING TO HAPPEN NEXT!**

It's a question we'd all still like to have answered.

Postcard by Donald McGill

THE ESSENTIAL FURNITURE

... 'Henrieta,' said Henry gravely, 'don't absolutely compel me to kiss you in the middle of Oxford Street in broad daylight.'

'But we've got to give it all up!'

'Got to what? Look here, kiddie, we are going immediately now to lunch together. But first take a glance round and tell me what you see.'

'Oh, shops and things. Daffodils in one of them.'

'I know, and the daffodils flattered themselves that they were pretty until you came past. Well, what you see I see as part of a place called the earth, and the books say there's a good deal more of it and some of it is not quite so crowded. Don't worry about flats. And I'm not worrying about the essential furniture. I thought that fumed oak, and inlaid tulip-wood, and upholstery, and a kitchen dresser with the ball-and-claw attachment of the period, had something to do with it. That was through talking to our Mr. Connon Ikestein.'

'Do I know him?'

'No, and I hope you never will. I was wrong, and he was wrong. Your house agents were wrong, and you were wrong. I'll tell you the true gospel, kiddie, for the look in your eyes revealed it to me.'

'What is it?

'There is this earth, and we who love are its essential furniture – all that the earth needs. Damn all price-lists. Am I to break my heart for a house agent? Are you to stand outside, the real, real life because of the price of a coal-scuttle? We are not going to give it up, kiddie. They may do what they like. They may swindle us, wreck us, and in the end starve us, but by the God that made us, we'll be happy first!'

And with this absurd project, totally wanting in resonable foresight, she expressed complete agreement. But not in words – for if she had spoken, she might have begun to cry, and one does not cry in Oxford Street.

The New Illustrated, 15 February 1919